ULLENHAL
Life after Lady Luxborough

To Carole

from Margaret

11/12/93

~ULLENHALL~

Life after Lady Luxborough

by

Margaret Feeney

BREWIN BOOKS

First published in November 1993
by K.A.F. Brewin Books,
Studley, Warwickshire. B80 7LG

ISBN 1 85858 026 9

Typeset in 11pt. Baskerville.
Made and printed in Great Britain by
Supaprint (Redditch) Ltd

Barrells Hall - severely damaged by fire
in April 1933

ACKNOWLEDGEMENTS

Mrs Carole Holt

Mrs Gladys Brockenshire

Mrs Dorothy Duckworth

Mrs Flo Lamb

Mr & Mrs K Portman

Mrs Norma Thursfield

Ken Earle

Mrs Mavis Gee

Mr Gordon Hemming

Mrs Celia Lewis

The late Mary Pugh

The late Mrs E. Friend

Mr Miles McNair

Shakespeare Trust Records Office

Oldberrow House - Nr Ullenhall

CONTENTS

THE ORIGINS OF ULLENHALL

The origins of Ullenhall go far back in the mists of time. It is generally believed that the original settlement dates back to Anglo-Saxon times with the Hale of Ullen (house or hall) of Chieftain Ulla being transformed with variations into the later spelling of Ullenhall. Many more houses are thought to have existed at Blunts Green and Deans Green and Hall End, with the Old Chapel on the hill making a central point.

During Edward the Confessor's reign in England a Saxon Thane called Waga or Wagen held the Manorship but he was dispossessed of the land and at Wootten by William the Conqueror who granted them to a relative, a Robert de Stafford. The settlement was then called Holehale.

When the Domesday Book was drawn up by William the Conqueror, England was already divided into counties and the counties into districts called hundreds. When facts were being collected for the Domesday Book, each hundred made its own inquiries through a group of people known as a 'jury'. All members took an oath to discover the truth. The information was passed to the Kings Officials at the County Court and then to the writers of the Domesday Book. This system of fact finding by officials of the King and a jury sworn to tell the truth later became the method used to try cases in the courts of law.

When the Domesday Book was drawn up it was said to be so thorough that there was not a single hide nor rod of land, not an ox, cow or pig left out.

In 1348 the Plague or Black Death reached England from Europe and almost every part of England and Wales was affected. It is thought that the original settlement of Ullenhall around the Old Chapel was decimated by the Plague and that new dwellings began on the site of today's Ullenhall village.

THE OLD CHAPEL

The chapel stands on high ground overlooking pleasant countryside and is thought to date from the 13th century. The nave was removed in 1876 because it was in an unstable condition and only a part of the original building remains. Originally there was a nave and chancel without aisles but when the nave was removed an older doorway was found in the wall presumably from an earlier church on the same site. The design of mouldings and carvings uncovered demonstrate that an earlier church may date to the 12th century. Beneath layers of whitewash, coloured decorations and passages from the Scriptures are thought to be taken from an earlier Bible than 1611.

There is a gallery at the west end where Sunday School children sat and musicians accompanied the hymns and psalms on the fiddle and flute. A bassoon was purchased in 1766, a hautboy in 1792 and two bassoon reeds in 1822. A clerk sat in the bottom of the three decked pulpit to lead the responses.

The wrought iron altar rails have the inscription J. Ward and T. Williams, 1735, the names of the churchwardens. In Hannett's 'Forest of Arden' the communion rails were said to be modern and the wrought iron rails were being used as a balustrade to the stairs of the gallery at the west end. Mr A.C. Coldicott, agent to the Barrells Estate found the rails in the woodyard at Barrells and Mr H.G. Newton had them replaced in 1919.

There are many other interesting features in the chapel and monuments to some notable people who have had connections with Ullenhall.

The sexton in the early 1900's was Mr Ben Franklin who lived in one of the cottages by the Old Chapel. He dug the graves at Ullenhall and Morton Bagot, also going to Tanworth, sometimes helped by his eldest sister Emma.

The funeral bier was kept in a shed at the back of the cottages. At Ullenhall Church (St. Mary's) he would help to start the singing, then take the collection plate round until Rev Whittaker organised churchwardens.

THE OLD CHURCH ULLENHALL.

LADY LUXBOROUGH

The life of Lady Luxborough and her residence at Barrells Hall have captured the imagination of many people down the ages. She was said to have a poetic and artistic temperament through the French blood in her veins. She was born in 1699, the youngest child of Henry Viscount St. John of Battersea and his French wife Angelica. She was on affectionate and goodwill terms with her half-brother Lord Bolingbroke, who was Minister of State to Queen Anne. Handel is reputed to have taught her music. She enjoyed verse making and reading English, French and Italian poetry.

Lady Luxborough

On the 10th June 1727 she married Robert Knight, son of the Robert Knight who was cashier of the South Sea Company. This was a successful trading company which led to great speculation in its shares, while other worthless companies were being formed to attract speculators, making shares soar above their real value. Eventually the South Sea 'Bubble' burst ruining many speculators. Robert Knight Snr. fled to the continent with a price on his head, but later obtained a pardon and returned to this country.

The marriage of Robert (Jnr) and Henrietta Knight was not a success. Henrietta was alleged to have had an affair with John Dalton a tutor to Lord Beauchamp, although she insisted that the friendship was merely platonic. This caused a scandal in society and she was banished to Barrells Hall in 1736, forbidden to travel within twenty miles of London and not allowed to see her two children. While in residence at Barrells she made some improvements to the house and took a great delight in creating a garden, with a Hermitage, a bowling green, Pheasant Yards, a Summerhouse, the making of a Ha-Ha, planting trees to line the walks, also placing many statues and urns in the grounds, with a Piping Faun in a double oak tree. She made friends among the local gentry, among them being Lord and Lady Archer of Umberslade and Lord and Lady Plymouth of Hewell, and kept up a good correspondence with many people. She became part of a small literary coterie, amongst them being poets William Shenstone, William Somervile, Richard Jago and Richard Graves.

the chapel at Wootton Wawen, then later moved to the Mausoleum in Barrells Park when it was built.

The Earl of Catherlough

Lord Catherlough's Mausoleum

Lord Luxborough was later created Earl of Catherlough and he was responsible for building the Mausoleum. When he died on 30th March 1772 he was also buried there.

The Earl of Catherlough had two children by his first wife Henrietta, Henry and Henrietta but they both died before their father. He married again but his second wife remained childless. During this time he met Jane Davies who lived at Moat House Farm, Ullenhall. Her father owed him a good deal of rent. He thought his steward had been too lenient and determined to call at the farm himself to tell the farmer Mr Davies, he must pay or be turned out. Instead he forgave him all rent and arrears when he fell in love with his daughter Jane. Her beauty of face and form had bewitched him. He persuaded her to join him at his house in London and provided several masters to teach her dancing, music, and French. During this time she bore him four children and later changed her name by deed poll to Knight. The eldest child Robert Knight succeeded to Barrells Hall and trustees were appointed until he became of age. In 1791 Robert Knight married and decided to enlarge Barrells. The architect Joseph Bonomi was employed and an elegant porte-cochere was designed by him to be added to the front of the building.

In 1830 Robert Knight authorised the removal of the Mausoleum in Barrells Park and the building of a vault at Ullenhall Chapel.

1830. From George Coppage to Robert Knight.

Oct. 15. Myself 1 day at 3/4d.	3 - 4
Labourer 1 day at 1/8d.	1 - 8
Oct. 23. Myself 6½ days at 3/8d.	£1 - 3 - 10
Bricklayer ½ day at 3/4d.	1 - 8
Labourer 6½ days at 2/-	13 - 6
Boy 3½ days at 1/2d.	4 - 1
Similar other items from Oct 30th to Nov 3rd	£8 - 7 - 3

	£10 - 15 - 4

Documents of title

Documents relating to sundry parcels of the settled estates, part of those which after disentailing passed to the Rev. H.C. Knight. These represent only a small proportion of the deeds and papers handed over by the trustees at that time (see no. 107). The deeds are here arranged in order of acquisition of the properties by Robert, earl of Catherlough or, after his death, by the trustees of the settled estates (see no. 81). Purchases nos. 1-7 were made in the Earl's lifetime, purchases nos. 8-32 were made by the trustees between 1776 and 1837.

Places for which no county is specified are in Warwickshire. Oldberrow was formerly in Worcestershire, being transferred to Warwickshire in 1896. Shipston (Worcestershire) and Clifford Chambers (Gloucestershire) were transferred to Warwickshire in 1931.

The Catherlough Arms, Henley-in-Arden

1-2. 4-5 December 1771

Lease and release, the release being a conveyance from William Mister of Shipston-upon-Stower co. Worcs. surgeon, devisee under the will of Elizabeth Wheatley late of Shipston-upon-Stower spinster deceased, and Mary his wife to the Rt.Hon. Robert earl of Catherlough, Viscount Barrells, Baron Luxborough of Shannon in the kingdom of Ireland, K.B., in consideration of £540 paid to William Mister, and £150 paid at his request to Sarah Pitt of Old Stratford spinster in discharge of a mortgage, of three messuages and a malthouse in Henley-in-Arden and 8 acres of land occupied therewith, then in the several occupations of Thomas Tibbatts, Edward Graves and Abraham Winspur.

The mortgage was made on 31 January 1723 to Edward Caddick for 1000 years and assigned at various dates to John Austin, to Elizabeth Tomes and to Sarah Pitt decd.

On discharge of the principal money to Sarah Pitt, sole executrix of Sarah Pitt decd., the residue of the term of years was assigned to Joseph Cruttenden gent. in trust for the said Robert earl of Catherlough.

Signed and sealed: William Mister, Mary Mister.
Seals applied on green silk: a swan gorged with a coronet.
Witnesses: Wm. Hunt, Robt. Crofts [clerk to Mr. Hunt].
Endorsed with acknowledgement of receipt of purchase money, same witnesses.

With certificate of registration of contract for redemption of land-tax, no. 14,774, dated 9 May 1799, pasted on verso of first membrance (see no. 75).

Endorsed: Purchase No. 7
             Premises at Henley late the Arms public house and 8 acres of land in the holding of —— White.

21.   24[-25] February 1779

Lease only of possession [release of 25 February 1779 lacking] from Edward Knight jun. of Wolverley co. Worcs. esq. devisee and trustee named in the will of Benjamin Palmer late of Olton in Solihull esq. decd. , William Richard Wilson of Solihull esq. and Jane Ann Eleanor his wife, one of the heirs at law of the said Benjamin Palmer, Henry Greswold Lewis of Malvern Hall in Solihull esq. and the Rev. Henry Wigley of Pensham co. Worcs. clerk, the two other heirs at law of the said Benjamin Palmer, to Thomas Fisher of Springfield House in Hampton-in-Arden esq. of the manor of Ulnall otherwise Ullenhall with the capital messuage or manor house known as the Hall and sundry closes and parcels of meadow, pasture, arable and woodland (names specified), except the Hop Yard close [&c.], the whole containing 205 acres 2 roods 13 perches, to hold for one whole year at a peppercorn rent to enable him to accept a release of the same to be made on the day following between the said Edward Knight jun. of the first part, the said W.R. Wilson, J.A.E. Wilson, H.G. Lewis and Henry Wigley of the second part, Charles Baldwyn of Aqualate co. Staffs. esq. and Elizabeth his wife of the third part, and the said Thomas Fisher of the fourth part.

Signed and sealed by the lessors.
Five armorial seals applied on green silk:
1.   indistinct
2.   a chevron between 3 mullets of 6 points, impaling a (?) wolf passant and in chief three mullets
3.   the same
4.   no impression
5.   a fess and in chief two greyhounds courant
Witnesses: R. Moland, Hugford Hassall, Fras. Hutton, Grays Inn.

Endorsed: Lands in Ullenhall purchased to the uses of the will of Earl Catherlough decd., 1873.
[Purchase No. 32]

The settled estates - their disentailing and sale

22.   18 June 1808

Printed Act of Parliament, 48 George III cap. 117, being an act for vesting certain estates in cos. Warwick, Middlesex and Montgomery, late of the Rt. Hon. Robert earl of Catherlough deceased, in trustees, in trust to be sold; and for investing the money arising from the sale thereof in the purchase of other estates, to be settled to the subsisting uses of the will of the said Robert earl of Catherlough, and for other purposes.

Recites the will of Robert earl of Catherlough dated 11 February 1772, whereby after charging his estates in various counties with the payment of an annuity of £400 to Jane Davies (since deceased) for her life, to be reduced to £100 in case of her marriage, and after charging his Edstone estate with the payment of an annuity of £300 to Henry Ralegh Knight, his second son by Jane Davies, for his life, he devised all his estates to trustees to the use of Robert Knight, his first son by Jane Davies, and his sons in tail male, with remainder to the use of Henry Ralegh Knight and his sons, and thereafter to the use of testator's daughters by Jane Davies, Jane Davies otherwise Knight and Henrietta Matilda Knight and their sons successively.   The Act recites also a codicil to the said will dated 24 February 1772 regarding the purchase of an estate from Newsam Peers esq., and that testator died on 30 March

8

1772, leaving the said Robert Knight, Henry Ralegh Knight, Jane Knight and Henrietta Knight as his only surviving children, of whom Robert Knight was the first tenant in tail, and recites the marriage settlement dated 9 June 1791 of Robert Knight and the Hon. Frances Dormer spinster, one of the daughters of Charles, Lord Dormer, and that the marriage took place on 12 June 1791, and that they had issue one son, Henry Knight, who had since died an infant without issue, and two daughters then living, Frances Elizabeth Knight and Georgiana Knight, while Jane Knight had married first Benjamin Bond Hopkins, and secondly Charles Fuller, and Henrietta Matilda Knight had married, and was then the widow of Michael Impey. The Act refers to the fact that several of the estates subject to the will of Robert earl of Catherlough lay in the county of Warwick lay detached from the family mansion of Barrells, and some in the counties of Middlesex and Montgomery at a very considerable distance, whereon it was proposed, and enacted, that these estates (specified in schedule 1) should be vested in George Wingfield Sparrow esq. and William Wingfield esq. as trustees for sale, the monies arising to be paid into the Bank of England in the name of the Accountant General of the High Court of Chancery, and afterwards laid out in the purchase of estates more conveniently placed. After the sale of the manor of Edstone, Henry Ralegh Knight's annuity of £300 was to be charged on other properties (specified in schedule 2).

Among other powers, including power to appoint new trustees, it was provided (section X) that in case the tenant for life and the first tenant in tail for the time being should signify in writing their desire that no more sales be made, then the trusts for sale under the Act should cease.

Schedule 1. Estates in Studley, Chadshunt and Edstone, co. Warwick, and in cos. Middlesex and Montgomery.
Schedule 2. Estates comprising the manor of Oldborough [Oldberrow] co. Worcs. and the manor of Barrells, co. Warwick, the latter including:

Barrells farm   in Ullenhall & Wootton Wawen
Crowleys farm   ''
Heath farm   ''
The Catherlough Arms in Ullenhall Street and a small house late the Catherlough Arms
Hill farm, Mount Pleasant, in Wootton Wawen
The Park farm in Beaudesert
The Park, the Bell inn and lands in Henley

23.   25 May 1833

Office copy decree of the High Court of Chancery appointing George Digby Wingfield of Lincolns Inn co. Middx. esq. and Richard Baker Wingfield of the Middle Temple, London, esq. trustees of the settled estates subject to the will of the late Earl of Catherlough, under the Act of 1808.

24.   28 July - 17 November 1854

Office copy will and codicil of those dates of Robert Knight of Barrells co. Warwick and of Grosvenor Square in Westminster esq. as follows:
Expenses of funeral not to exceed £100.
Remains to be placed in vault under family pew at Chadshunt.
Three calendar months' wages to each of his domestic servants.
To his butler Joseph Sharpe an annuity of £25 for life, to be allowed him by testator's daughter Frances Elizabeth Knight and after her decease by his daughter Georgiana King, wife of Edward Bolton King esq.

9

To Robert Myddelton Biddulph of Chirk Castle co. Denbigh esq., Lt.-Col. Thomas Myddelton Biddulph, Master of the Queen's Household, and Richard Baker Wingfield of the Middle Temple esq. all his reduced 3 per cent annuities in trust to pay the annual proceeds to his daughter Frances Elizabeth Knight for life, and after her decease to his daughter Georgiana King, and after her decease to such of his 7 grand-children (King) as should survive him and attain the age of 21 years. To the same R.M. Biddulph and T.M. Biddulph the Upper Marlborough close in Studley and a close adjoining occupied by Widow Priest, in trsut for the same purposes as were specified for certain other freehold estates in Studley and Ipsley by indenture dated 28 March 1850 between himself and the same trustees.

To his daughter Frances Elizabeth Knight the tithe rent-charge of £4 per annum charged on the Boblake close in Studley, his freehold messuage in Grosvenor Square in which he then lived and all the residue of his real and personal estate absolutely.

In the event of her (Frances's) death in his lifetime, these bequests to go to his daughter Georgiana King, and the event of her (Georgiana's) death to his son-in-law Edward Bolton King.

He appointed his daughter Frances Elizabeth Knight sole executrix, and in the event of her death his daughter Georgiana King.

Dated: 28 July 1854.   Signed: R. Knight.
Witnesses: Richard Williams banker, Pall Mall East, James Flowers clerk to Messrs. Ransome & Co. Pall Mall East.

Codicil dated 17 November 1854.

To his daughter Georgiana King all arrears of rent owing at his decease from the messuages and lands in Chadshunt and Gaydon whereof he was tenant for life.
To Robert Myddelton Biddulph of Chirk Castle, £100.
To Colonel Thomas Myddelton Biddulph, £100.
To Richard Baker Wingfield, £100.
To his grandson Edward Raleigh King, £200.
To Mr. Edward Cooper of Henley-in-Arden land agent, £50.
To his butler Joseph Sharpe, £50.

On the death of his daughter Frances Elizabeth Knight the four pictures (specified) to be taken to Chadshunt and given to his daughter Georgiana King.

Dated and signed as above.
Witnesses: Thos. Layton, 14 Moore Street, Chelsea, and 60 Piccadilly, James L. Stockley, 53 Sydney Street, Brompton, and 60 Piccadilly.

Proved at London with a codicil, 1 February 1855.

25.   6 January 1855

Deed poll for determining the trusts for sale under the Act of 1808 (no. 22 above) being a declaration by Charles Raleigh Knight of 36 Montague Square co. Middx. esq. late a captain in Her Majesty's 25th regiment of infantry, reciting the will of Robert earl of Catherlough dated 11 February 1772, whereby after providing for the pay-ment of certain annuities he devised all his estates in trust to the use of his eldest son Robert Knight for life, and to his sons in order of seniority in tail male, with remainder to his second son Henry Raleigh Knight and his sons likewise, and a codicil to the same dated 24 February 1772, and that testator died on 30 March 1772, and that Robert Knight married in 1791 the Hon. Frances Dormer spinster, who died in 1842 having had issue by him three children, viz. Henry Knight who was born 179[ ] and died an infant without issue, Frances Elizabeth Knight and Georgiana Knight, and that Henry Raleigh Knight married in 18[ ] Juliana Bolton spinster and died in 1836, having had issue by her four children viz. Henry Raleigh Knight jun. who died 18[ ] an infant and unmarried, the said Charles Raleigh Knight his only other son and two daughters, and reciting the Act of 1808, and that Robert Knight died on 5 January 1855 without leaving issue male as aforesaid, and

10

no accounts having been rendered to him of the real and personal estates devised under the will of 1772, he the said Charles Raleigh Knight as surviving son of Henry Raleigh Knight and in pursuance of powers contained in the Act of 1808, declared the trusts for sale relating to such of the estates as then remained unsold to be determined and at an end, and directed the trustees to convey the said estates to the uses of the will of Robert earl of Catherlough.

Signed and sealed: C.R. Knight.
Seal applied on green silk.
Witnesses: Wm. Parke, 63 Lincoln's Inn Fields, solr., Thos. Elmes clerk to Mr. Wm. Parke.

26.   8 January 1855

Disentailing deed being a release in fee from Charles Raleigh Knight (as above) to William Parke of No. 63 Lincolns Inn Fields co. Middx. gent., reciting the will of Robert earl of Catherlough dated 11 February 1772 and a codicil dated 24 February 1772, and that testator died on 30 March 1772, and reciting that Robert Knight had married Frances Dormer spinster and by her had three children, and that Henry Raleigh Knight had married Juliana Bolton spinster and by her had four children, including the said Charles Raleigh Knight his only surviving son (as above), and reciting the Act of 1808, and the death of Robert Knight on 5 January 1855, and the declaration (no. 25 above) dated 6 January 1855, and that he as surviving son of the said Henry Raleigh Knight was or claimed to be entitled to an estate in tail male in all the real estates subject to the will of Robert earl of Catherlough, and being desirous of having the said estates discharged from entail and vested in him absolutely, it was then witnessed that the said Charles Raleigh Knight conveyed to the said William Parke free of entail all the said manors, messuages and lands, and assigned to him all the monies and personal estate intended to be laid out in purchase of such estates under the will of 1772 or Act of 1808, in trust for the said Charles Raleigh Knight.

Signed and sealed: C.R. Knight.
Seal applied on green silk.
Witnesses: Thos. Elms, Chas. Twort, clerks to Mr. Wm. Parke.   Endorsed as having been enrolled in the High Court of Chancery, 12 January 1855.

27.   9 January 1855

Deed poll for determining the trusts for sale under the Act of 1808 (no. 22 above) being a declaration by the Rev. Henry Charles Knight late of Bognor co. Sussex but then of Oak Hill House, Cowes, Isle of Wight, clerk, reciting the will of Robert earl of Catherlough dated 11 February 1772, and codicil dated 24 February 1772, and that testator died on 30 March 1772, and that Robert Knight married in 1791 the Hon. Frances Dormer spinster, who died in 1842 having had issue four children viz. Henry Knight born 179[ ] and died an infant without issue, Frances Elizabeth Knight, Georgiana Knight and the said Henry Charles Knight, born 1813, and reciting the Act of 1808, and that Robert Knight died on 5 January 1855 without having been again married, and no accounts having been rendered to him of the real and personal estates devised under the will of 1772 or of the sales and purchases under the Act of 1808, he the said Henry Charles Knight as surviving son of Robert Knight and in pursuance of powers contained in the said Act, declared the trusts for sale relating to such of the estates as then remained unsold to be at an end, and directed the trustees to convey the same to the uses of the will of Robert earl of Catherlough.

Signed and sealed: Henry Charles Knight.
Seal applied on green silk.
Witnesses: Lewis W. Miller, James Elms, clerks to Mr. William Parke.

Note.   Appears to have been signed 'Charles Knight' and the name 'Henry' added in the same hand.

According to this, the former claimed to be entitled to an estate in tail male expectant on the death of Robert Knight, the first life tenant under the will of Robert earl of Catherlough decd., in regard to the real and personal property subject to the said will or to the Act of 1808 (no. 22 above), and to an absolute interest in the family heirlooms, but Charles Raleigh Knight denied such claim and himself claimed to be entitled to the same estate and interest, whereon in order to avoid litigation and disputes, the said H.C. Knight and C.R. Knight had agreed to vest all the said real and personal estates and heirlooms in trustees, to be disposed of for the benefit of both parties.

They agreed that, if both of them should survive the said Robert Knight, they should take all necessary steps to discharge the real estates from entail and the monies from trusts under the will, codicil or Act, and to vest them in two trustees, one to be nominated by each party, and should any estates remain unsold to determine the trusts for sale and vest them in the same trustees, upon the following trusts.

All real estates and personal estate not consisting of monies were to be sold, and from one equal moiety of the proceeds a sum of £15,000 was to be raised for the absolute benefit of and paid to C.R. Knight, the balance of that moiety to be in trust for H.C. Knight and the other moiety in trust for C.R. Knight.   In the meantime one moiety of all rents and income arising was to be applied first to raise interest at the rate of 3 per cent on C.R. Knight's £15,000 and the residue in trust for H.C. Knight, and the other moiety in trust for C.R. Knight.

After reciting that Robert Knight died on 5 January 1855 without having again been married, the deed of management recites an indenture of even date but of prior execution (of which no. 29 is a draft) between (1) Henry Charles Knight, (2) Charles Raleigh Knight, (3) William Parke, and (4) John Bullar and William Frederick Beadon, whereby in pursuance of the agreement of 19 January 1844, the two first estates, and William Parke, H.C. Knight and C.R. Knight assigned to the same all monies, personal estate and heirlooms, mentioned in the disentailing assurances of 8 and 10 January 1855 (nos. 26 & 28 above) as subject to the will and codicil of 1772 and Act of 1808, in trust to uses to be specified.

To specify these uses it was then witnessed that the said John Bullar and W.F. Beadon should stand seized of all the said estates and hereditaments in trust to divide them into two equal moieties, one moiety in trust for H.C. Knight but charged with a payment of £15,000 to C.R. Knight and the other moiety in trust for C.R. Knight, with certain provisos specified, the said John Bullar and W.F. Beadon to manage the real and personal estates in the intervening period until the trusts should have been fulfilled, with full power to open and work mines, fell timber, cut underwood, erect or pull down houses or other buildings, repair Barrells mansion house, sell materials, make or close roads, plant trees and hedges, make new divisions of fields, drain lands, insure property against loss or damage by fire &c.

37.   24 June 1857

Conveyance from John Bullar and W.F. Beadon (as above) to the Rev. H.C. Knight (as above), reciting the indenture of 5 April 1855 above recited, and that they had contracted with him for the sale of certain tithes, in consideration of the sum of £1,000, of all the great and rectorial tithes or rentcharges in lieu on lands in Wootton Wawen parish specified in the schedule annexed, to hold to the said H.C. Knight and his heirs for ever, subject to the payment of £9.5s.4d. per annum to the vicar of Wootton Wawen and of £6 per annum to the minister of Bearley, the said H.C. Knight declaring against any entitlement of his wife to dower in the same.

Schedule showing owners' names, quantities and rentcharges.

Signed and sealed by the grantors.
Seals: no significant impression.
Witness: Francis T. Bircham, solr., Parliament St., Westminster.
Endorsed with memorandum of receipt of consideration money, same witness.
[Lot no. 16]

37a. [24 June] 1857

Copy draft of the same, the Rev. H.C. Knight's address being given as 'Holly Lodge, Leamington', with the words 'Holly Lodge' crossed through, subscribed in red ink as approved on behalf of Mr. Bullar and Mr. Beadon by M. Elwin, Lincolns Inn, 2 June 1857.   Also original draft in which Mr. Knight is described as of Oak Hill house, West Cowes, signed by H. Thring, 17 December 1856.

The Rev. H.C. Knight's estate

41. 29 September 1859

Draft conveyance from the Rev. H.C. Knight of Leamington clerk to James Salt of Ullenhall publican and his trustee Edwin Eugene Whitaker of Lincolns Inn Fields co. Middx. gent., reciting the conveyance dated 24 June 1857 from John Bullar and W.F. Beadon to H.C. Knight and an agreement to purchase between James Salt and H.C. Knight, in consideration of the sum of £250, of the messuage and premises known as the Spur inn, Ullenhall, fronting the road from Beoley to Henley-in-Arden and then in James Salt's occupation, to hold to the said James Salt to such uses as he should specify and failing any such, to the use of E.E. Whitaker in trust for James Salt; the latter declared against entitlement of his wife to dower.

Sketch-plan annexed.

42. 1 August 1884

Memorandum that by indenture dated 1 August 1884 the Rev. H.C. Knight in consideration of £10 conveyed to Edward Charles Browning, William York Marston and Charles Callow Smith, trustees of a settlement therein referred to, a piece of land at Henley-in-Arden near the Bear inn and then used as garden ground therewith, bounded on the South side by a lane leading from the village towards certain fields belonging to H.C. Knight, on the East by the said Bear inn and on other sides by property of George Bullivant and others, to hold to the said trustees upon the trusts of the said settlement.

Couchman & Son, solrs., Henley-in-Arden, 2 August 1884.

43. 5 January 1886

Copy will of that date of the Rev. Henry Charles Knight of Heathlands, Malvern Wells co. Worcs. clerk in holy orders.   Appoints his friends Charles Roger Jacson of Barton Hall near Preston co. Lancs. esq., Arnold More at present residing in London a lieutenant-colonel in H.M. Army and the Rev. Frederick Peel clerk in holy orders of Barassie House, Malvern Link, vicar of Little Malvern co. Worcs. to be executors and trustees.
Bequests as follows:
To each of his trustees £50;
To such of his daughters as should be spinsters at the time of his decease £600 and all his jewelry, plate furniture, china, glass, pictures and contents of his house and garden;
To Edwin Evelyn Dormer of Henley-in-Arden esq. an annuity of £100 for life;
To his sister-in-law Emma Margaret Minchin of Cliff Cottage, West Cowes, I.O.W., an annuity of £7.10s.0d. for life;
To his servant Caroline Medley if she should survive all his daughters an annuity of £50 for life; these three annuities to be free of legacy duty;
All his messuages, farms and lands in Wootton Wawen, his dwelling-house called Heathlands and all other real estate he left to his trustees in trust for sale;

Robert Knight

44.   20 May 1818

Copy memorandum of agreement made on that day between Robert Knight of Barrels esq. and Henry Taylor of Freemans Green in Ullenhall carpenter, whereby the said Robert Knight in consideration of the said Henry Taylor undertaking to erect a cottage on part of a pleck of ground opposite the Catherlough Arms public house in Ullenhall, agreed to allow all materials that could be found from old buildings on Crowlies farm then pulled down and the sum of £20 for workmanship and for other necessary materials, and to grant a lease of such new cottage with a suitable garden for 21 years at an annual rent of 5s. payable quarterly from June 24 then following, if the said Henry Taylor, his mother Mary Taylor and his then wife Hannah or one of them should so long live.

Henry Taylor agreed not to yield up possession of the premises to any one without consent in writing of Robert Knight, and he further agreed in consideration of an additional £15 to be paid him by Robert Knight to pull down his then dwelling at Freemans Green and yield up possession of his garden and site there forthwith.

Signed: R. Knight, Henry Taylor.
Witnesses: Thos. Pepper servant of Robert Knight,
             Edw. Cooper   )
) Henley-in-Arden.
             Thos. Cooper jun.)

45.   4 April 1845

Agreement between Robert Knight of Barrels esq. and Edward Cooper of Henley-in-Arden for lease to the latter of a farm called Fosters and Shreeves closes in Ullenhall and a messuage then used as offices with several enclosures of pasture land, orchard and outbuildings in Henley-in-Arden then in the occupation of the said Edward Cooper, except timber, mines and quarries and game, to hold for one whole year at six months' notice at a yearly rent of £122, paying also £100 p.a. for every acre of meadow or pasture ploughed up for tillage, and the same for every acre sowed with flax, rape, hemp or other pernicious seeds, with husbandry conditions (specified), the tenant to do two days customary labour for the landlord yearly with a team of four horses, a man and a boy, not more than 14 miles from the premises.

Signed: R. Knight, Edw. Cooper.
Witness: Bolton King.

Schedule of lands with description and quantity, amounting to 42a. 3r. 3p. arable and 32a. 3r. 20p. meadow and pasture, total 75a. 2r. 23p.

Printed form completed in manuscript.

54.   [blank] 1872

Tenancy agreement from the Rev. H.C. Knight of Heathlands, Malvern Wells co. Worcs. clerk to Newton Pratt of Hatton Lodge farmer in respect of the farm known as Hall End farm in Ullenhall containing 222 acres, to hold from March 25th next for one year and so on from year to year, paying £321.18s.0d. per annum and an additional yearly rent of £20 for every acre of meadow or pasture converted to tillage, and of £20 for every timber tree cut down, without consent in writing.

Signed: H.C. Knight, Newton Pratt.
Witnesses: Frances K.S. Knight, daughter of Mr. Knight, Wm. Whitehouse.

Apparently executed but not dated.

55. 10 May 1875

Tenancy agreement from the Rev. H.C. Knight (as above) to George Edwin Rose Clarke of Haddington co. Oxon. farmer in respect of Fosters farm in Wootton Wawen containing 110 acres, to hold from 25 March 1875 for one year and so on from year to year at the yearly rent of £228, on similar conditions to those in no. 54.

Signed: Henry C. Knight, George Edwin Rose Clarke.
Witness: Wm. Wilkes Cawley, solr., Great Malvern.
Attached is no. 56.

56. 17 November 1876

Agreement between   1. George Edwin Rose Clarke,
                     2. Henry Charles Knight, and
                     3. George Britten of Wootton Wawen farmer,
whereby the first-named with the consent of the said H.C. Knight assigned to the said George Britten his tenancy of Fosters farm, Wootton Wawen, and the landlord agreed to let the same to George Britten from March 25th next on the same conditions as specified in no. 55.

Signed: George Edwin Rose Clarke, Henry C. Knight, George Britten.
Witnesses: Edwin Evelyn Dormer, Henrietta Knight daughter of H.C. Knight.
Attached to no. 55.

57. 18 September 1878

Agreement whereby Henry Forsters of Lower Skilts in Studley agreed to rent and take of the Rev. H.C. Knight the messuage and farm called Fosters farm in Wootton Wawen, then in the occupation of the landlord, on a yearly tenancy beginning 29 September 1878 at a rent of £166.10s.0d. per annum, subject to conditions specified.

Signed: Henry C. Knight, Henry Forster.
Witness: Frances Knight.
Schedule of lands with description and quantity.

Legal papers

The settled estates

58. May 1855

Copy preliminary report of Mr. Bircham to the Trustees in the form of a letter addressed to John Bullar and W.F. Beadon esquires.   Early in April he had engaged Mr. John Bailey Denton, with his partner Mr. Drake, to make a survey and valuation of the whole property.   He accompanied Messrs. Denton and Drake to Henley on April 13th and 14th.   They also had assistance from Mr. Cooper, agent of the late Mr. Knight.

Messrs. Denton & Co. would shortly submit a general plan.   The writer submitted a terrier.

Including Barrells House and Park the property in Warwickshire and Worcestershire comprised about 3020 acres, the woodland being principally in hand and the arable, pasture and meadow let in 17 holdings or farms.

The whole of the farms and woodlands lie together in Wootton Wawen (including Ullenhall, Aspley and Henley), Studley and Beaudesert in Warwickshire and Oldberrow in Worcestershire.

The tenants are held under written agreements from year to year.   Gross rental for 1854, £3,756.13s.0d.   Smaller holdings and cottages produced in gross £45 and tithe rent-charge in Ullenhall £59.14s.3d.

The mansion house appeared to have been largely built by the late Robert Knight in completion of a design by the late Earl Catherlough. The part built by the latter was then occupied as the village school room and as the residence of a labourer employed on the estate. The part built by Robert Knight had been uninhabited for 30 years and was in a lamentable state of dilapidation.

The site of the stabling was pointed out to them but this had all been pulled down. The walled garden was in complete decay and only traces of the glasshouses remained.

Little remained of the approach road from Henley and avenue of elms and nothing of the entrance lodge. These elms may however have decayed through natural causes.

Towards Ullenhall Robert Knight had made a new approach road across the park with a lodge on each side of it. The road remained but the lodges had disappeared.

The mausoleum mentioned in Lord Catherlough's will had fallen out of repair and had been ransacked by thieves, and Robert Knight had removed its contents to Ullenhall chapel and pulled down the mausoleum altogether.

The writer would take counsel's opinion of the question of waste.

The farm buildings were for the most part in miserable condition, due no doubt to the system of letting from year to year, while exacting the utmost rent and doing the least possible repairs.

Apart from the timber in Barrells Park there was no timber worth speaking of, fit to cut for repairs or sale.

Robert Knight had pulled down farm buildings and cottages, but no doubt with the intention of improvement at the time.

Besides the Warwickshire and Worcestershire estates, the settled estates under the will of Lord Catherlough included the fee simple of tithe commutation rentcharges payable in the parish of Mold, Flintshire. According to Mr. Cooper's report, these produced gross in 1854, £1,538.18s.5d. payable by about 500 different landowners, and rates and expenses of collection in that year amounted to £330.2s.4d. leaving a nett sum of £1,208.16s.1d.

Lord Catherlough's will being dated 17 February 1772 and codicil 24 February 1772, and probate being granted 10 April 1772, it was improbable that anything devised by the will should have been disposed of in the interval, but the will devised manors, lands &c. not only in cos. Warwick, Worcester and Flint but also in cos. Lincoln, Middlesex, Salop and Chester.

So far no trace had been found of any lands in Lincolnshire or Salop.

In Middlesex Lord Catherlough had a house in Golden Square which was sold under the powers of the Act of 1808.

As regards the Cheshire property, an explanation was forthcoming which would also apply to the 'heirloom' and the Flintshire tithes.

At the time of his death Lord Catherlough had no real estate in these two counties except an estate at Tarvin co. Chester and at Llwynegrin and the rectorial tithes of Mold co. Flint which he held for the remainder of a foreclosed mortgage term of 1,000 years.

There were Chancery proceedings about this property and about the heirlooms in a suit instituted by the late Robert Knight in 1803 against his brother and his own then surviving children (the present Miss Knight and Mrs. King) for the purpose of obtaining a declaration that, as administrator and sole legal personal representative of his infant son then lately dead, he was absolutely entitled to the mortgage term and the heirlooms - see Decree made 26 January 1806.

Having obtained this declaration, Robert Knight would be able to dispose of the property in question.

Portions of the estates in cos. Warwick and Worcester were sold under the Act of 1808.

The Montgomeryshire estates were sold in the same way.

The estates settled to the uses of Lord Catherlough's will could be classed as follows:
(1)   those being his Lordship's property at the time of his death;
(2)   those purchased with the produce of his real and personal residuary estate; and
(3)   those purchased with the produce of sales under the Act of 1808.

The greatest portion of the then estate would be found in class 3.

The Act of 1808 was passed on the suggestion that the Earl's will contained no powers of sale, and that the estates in other parts of Warwickshire were not convenient to hold with the family mansion of Barrells.

The writer had obtained a copy of the Act account from the Court of Chancery and found that every penny paid in from sales had been paid out again for new purchases.

The principal purchasers had been Robert Knight himself and his son-in-law Bolton King, so that some of the sales and purchases had been virtually exchanges.

The writer had sent copies of this preliminary report to Mr. Whitaker and Mr. Parke.

Signed by Francis T. Bircham.

58a.   12 March 1857

Copy letter from the Inland Revenue Office, Somerset House, to Bircham & Co. about estates of the late Robert earl of Catherlough in Lincolnshire, no trace of which could then be found.   Bircham & Co. had referred to a report that these had been sold by Robert Knight, the life tenant, under the powers of the land tax Acts and the produce applied in redeeming land tax on other part of the estates.

The Inland Revenue Office replied that all deeds of conveyance of estates in England sold for the redemption of land tax (where consideration exceeded £200) were required to be enrolled or registered within 6 months, and that on examination being made, no conveyance of estates in Lincolnshire by Robert Knight were found to have been registered in the books of that office.

It was also the case that estates sold for the purpose mentioned were required by law to be conveyed free of land tax, and the contracts for redemption of land tax would therefore have been recorded in that office, but on search being made, the only contract which could be traced for redemption of land tax in Lincolnshire by Robert Knight was for the trifling sum of 10s.3d. in Grimsby.

Signed: E. Russell, deputy registrar.

59.   [May] 1855

In Chancery.   Transcript of accounts of the trustees of the will of the late Robert earl of Catherlough under the Act of 1808, exparte the purchasers of the estates, from the books of the Accountant-General, 1809-15.

Inscribed: Messrs. Bircham & Co. No.1
Note inside fron cover: 22.4.55...   2 books.

60.   [May] 1855

In Chancery.   Transcript of sundry accounts in the cause Knight v. Vane, from the books of the Accountant-General, 1780-1822.   Arranged in four series as follows:
(1)   In Master Ords office   1780-1805
(2)   The personal estate   1786-1822

(3)   The plaintiff Henry Raleigh Knight
                  the infants account   1789-90
(4)   The plaintiff Henrietta Matilda Knight
                  the infants account   1789-92

Inscribed: Messrs. Bircham & Co.
Note inside front cover: 25 April 1855.   24 openings.

61.   May 1855

Draft costs in Knight v. Richards.   Costs of entering satisfaction to judgement herein
registered on the 17 July 1843.   Total £4.12s.8d.
Includes item: Drawing affidavit of E.T. Whitaker in support of application....

62.   11 June 1855

Copy case exparte the Trustees of the estates formerly of the Earl of Catherlough
decd. as to waste, and opinion of Mr. G.M. Giffard.

The late tenant for life Mr. Robert Knight, who died on January 5th last, enjoyed the
estate for an unusually long period.

The Earl died in 1772, being seised in fee of the freehold estates and absolute owner
of certain chattels devised as heirlooms and of a chattel interest in a forfeited mortgage term in certain tithes in co. Flint.

By will he devised his estate to his illegitimate son Robert Knight, then an infant of
about 10 years, for life without impeachment of waste, and to his first and other
sons in tail, with remainder to testator's illegitimate son Henry Raleigh Knight for
life and to his sons in tail.

Robert Knight attained his majority on 3 March 1789 and entered into possession of
the estate.

On his death in 1855 Robert Knight left surviving him, besides two daughters, a son
[Henry Charles] whose legitimacy he disputed and a nephew (a son of his brother
H.R. Knight), who, failing the legitimacy of the son, would have succeeded to the
estates.

These two on Robert's death proceeded to disentail the estates and conveyed them
to trustees for management, sale and division between them on an agreed plan.

At the time of Robert's succession the estates consisted of Barrells and about 650
acres adjoining in cos. Warwick and Worcester, the manors and lands of Chadshunt,
Studley and Edstone, a freehold house in Golden Square [co. Middx.] and a large
estate in Montgomeryshire, of an annual value of c. £4,300 exclusive of tithes.

At this time there was a fine avenue of trees on the approach to Barrells, where
Robert Knight resided from time to time down to about 1825.

Shortly after he came of age he had made considerable alterations there in completion or continuation of a plan begun by the Earl, including a completely new
range of stabling.   This last he pulled down after ceasing to reside at Barrells.

In the same way he improved the gardens, enclosing them by a brick wall, and built
glasshouses &c.   These were all then dilapidated or gone.

He built a new road across the park and built two lodges, which had then also
disappeared.

Down to 1808 the trustees of the will of Earl Catherlough under sanction of the
Court of Chancery in an administration suit instituted shortly after Lord Catherlough's death made various purchases of lands, in part on Robert Knight's suggestion.
These included cottages &c. since pulled down.   By 1808 the annual gross value of
the settled estates, exclusive of tithes, was £5,211.

18

The will of Lord Catherlough contained no powers of sale, but in 1808 an Act was obtained giving the trustees powers to sell more than two thirds of the estate. These estates were sold for approximately £170,000 and the money paid into Chancery.

Between 1813 and 1836 the whole of this sum was laid out, with the sanction of the court, in the acquisition of sundry farms and premises in the vicinity of Barrells. The present gross annual rental of the estate (excluding tithes) was £3,756.

In several instances large sums were given for timber on the lands purchased.

In 1825 owing to family divisions and domestic troubles Robert Knight ceased to reside on the estate. He then pulled down the stabling and removed the materials to Ullenhall, and abandoned the mansion which was allowed to fall into great dilapidation.

Thieves at one time stripped the roof of its lead and water was allowed to enter for some time before the roof was re-covered with zinc.

With one or two exceptions the farm buildings on the estate were in a bad state of repair. The farms appear to have been let from year to year at the highest rent which could be exacted, with the least possible spent on repairs, this resulting in considerable depreciation of value of the estate.

Whatever the position in Barrells Park, more timber had been cut on the estate as a whole than could be reconciled with good husbandry.

On the death of Robert Knight, leaving a large residuary personal estate entirely alienated from the possessors of the Barrells estate, the question was whether any claim for waste could be maintained against the representatives of the late Robert Knight.

Whilst at Mold Mr. Porter saw the Dean of St. Asaph, who was formerly vicar of Mold, and gained the information that at some time immediately before their purchase for the trust estate, the tithes were offered for sale by Robert Knight to his (the Dean's) father at a price considerably less than £50,000, but that during the negotiations the offer was suddenly withdrawn.

Signed: Francis T. Bircham.   Undated.

64.   18 June 1855

Copy case exparte the Trustees of the estates of the Earl of Catherlough decd. as to the Mold tithes, and opinion of Mr. G.M. Giffard.

Counsel was furnished with documents including an abstract of deeds by which the tithe estates were annexed to the settled property and a copy of the decree in Chancery of 26 January 1806 by which a declaration was made respecting title to the same.

Mr. Robert Knight the tenant for life of the settled estates married in 1791 and not long after there were three children of the marriage, Henry a son who died at the age of 6 in 1800 and two daughters.

In 1803 Robert Knight, having taken out administration of the effects of his infant son, claimed as administrator to be absolutely entitled to the tithe estate.

These tithes were about 1730 mortgaged by the fee simple impropriator to the Earl of Plymouth for a term of 1000 years. The mortgage was afterwards foreclosed, the principal, interest and costs then due being between £12,000 and £13,000. The tithes in 1764 became vested in the Earl of Catherlough for the remainder of the term.

Robert Knight's claim to absolute ownership of the tithes was based on the plea that they passed by the general devise of real estates in his father's will, and being personalty, they vested absolutely in his son as the first tenant in tail, and on the son's death came to him as his father and sole next-of-kin.

The trustees of the will appear not to have acquiesced in this view, but Robert Knight filed his bill against them and obtained the decree of 1806.

The Earl's will contained no powers of sale but in 1808 Robert Knight applied to and obtained from Parliament powers to remedy this omission. Schedule 1 of the resulting Act listed the estates which it was then thought desirable to sell, and Schedule 2 those which it was proposed to retain. Neither schedule contained the Mold tithes, as these had been declared Robert Knight's property.

The total annual value of the then remaining settled estates appeared to be £5,210, of which three-quarters was represented by Schedule 1.

The proposed sales and new purchases were intended to produce a more compact estate in the immediate vicinity of Barrells. All the properties comprised in Schedule 1 were shortly afterwards sold, and the money paid into Chancery, and new properties purchased.

On Robert Knight's death the estates passed into the hands of trustees for management and division among the parties beneficially entitled to them.

A considerable difference was observed between the amounts realised by the estates sold under the Act of 1808 and the then value of the estate, which was reported to be less than was produced by the sale of the 1808 Schedule 1 properties alone.

A considerable portion of the estates sold under the Act of 1808 was sold either to Robert Knight himself or to his son-in-law Mr. Bolton King.

Before going further into these matters the Trustees sought the opinion of Counsel on the case of the Mold tithes, which was at least free from some of the difficulties affecting the rest of the estate.

It appeared that Lord Catherlough acquired these tithes for the residue of the mortgage term of 1,000 years for £13,000 and that other property came with them, particulars of which were unknown, that the remainder of the mortgage term was in 1806 decreed to be the absolute property of Robert Knight, that in 1808 the latter possessed himself of the reversion in the tithes for a nominal consideration, and that in 1810 Robert Knight sold and conveyed the tithes in fee simple to the trustees of the settled estates for £49,950, with the approval of the Court of Chancery.

In 1837 the tithes were commuted and in 1854 the gross amount of them was £1,691.12s.4d., but after rates and taxes and expenses of collection the nett amount received by the owners was under £1,210. The amounts receivable were very small, being payable by upwards of 400 tenants.

The difference between the value in 1855 and the purchase money in 1810 might be accounted for by the change in value of agricultural produce in this period, but at the 1810 figure the tithes could have been considerably over-valued.

Advice being taken by the trustees of J.B. Denton as to the then value of the tithes, the latter's opinion is quoted to the effect that, assuming £1,200 per annum to be the annual nett income of the estate after payment of expenses, the then value in fee simple was £26,660, this representing 21½ years' purchase. A lesser amount might be expected if the property were sold by auction. Tithes were in general more valuable before commutation, but this would not account for such a large sum as £49,950 being paid in 1810. If 25 per cent were added to the then value (making £34,000), this would represent the maximum value of the property.

Counsel was asked to advise whether there existed any sufficient grounds for impeaching the purchase of this tithe estate out of the trust funds.

Copy opinion

The sale of the tithes through the Court in the circumstances described was open to suspicion and worth the expense of further investigation.

Signed by George Markham Giffard, 2 Stone Buildings, Lincolns Inn, 18 June 1855.

65.   27 August 1856

Copy counsel's observations on the abstract of title to the tithes at Mold and on Captain Knight's proposed purchase thereof.

The abstract consisted solely of the conveyance from the late Robert Knight in June 1810.   The title was investigated and approved by the Court of Chancery at that time.   Absence of the title deeds (including the original grant) was however so suspicious that Captain Knight should not proceed in the purchase until they were accounted for.

Signed by C. Parke, 24 Old Square, Lincolns Inn, 27 August 1856.

The Rev. H.C. Knight's estate

66.   17 December 1856

Opinion on title of the Barrells estate by Harry Thring.

Counsel had perused the title to lots 6, 8, 11, 13, 14, 15 and 16 on behalf of the Rev. H.C. Knight.   The difficulty in this title consisted in the identification of the parcels;   in several instances three separate descriptions being furnished, (1) that of the particulars, (2) that in the abstract, and (3) that in the map.   The evidence with respect to the land tax being discharged was very defective and the purchaser should obtain a declaration on this point.   He had conveyed the tithes in lot 16 by a separate deed, as they could not conveniently be mixed up.

Signed: Harry Thring, 6 Old Buildings, Lincolns Inn, 17 December 1856.

67.   25 January 1862

Case and opinion of Mr. W.O. Edge regarding damage to a fence adjoining a former wheelwright's shop at Ullenhall.

The Rev. H.C. Knight was in possession of a considerable landed property in Ullen-hall derived under an entail created by the will of Lord Catherlough.   The small property concerned in the present case was one of those purchased by the trustees of the will by conveyance dated 1837, when it was described as a messuage or tenement with the wheelwright's shop, stable, yard, garden &c. then in the occu-pation of Thomas Dolphin.   The wheelwright's shop was afterwards used as a cowhouse.   Adjoining it was a piece of ground used by Dolphin as a timber yard. Dolphin occupied it first as owner and then for c. 50 years as Robert Knight's tenant.

A trumpery dispute arose about this piece of ground involving also Mr. Edward Cooper.   Mr. Cooper was tenant of Robert Knight's principal farm but, differences having arisen, he was then under notice to quit.   He was also agent for Kings College, Cambridge, the owners of the adjoining field.

While the wheelwright's business was continued the piece of ground was left open, but lately it had appeared more convenient to the then tenant, William Edwards, to inclose ie, and Robert Knight's agent directed him to do so.

Edward Cooper however, after first threatening Robert Knight's agent, proceeded with one Joseph Bench a surveyor on 19 November last [1861] to the place and directed him to saw off 8 posts and demolish the fence, which he did.

Note that Cooper had been not only tenant but als agent to Robert Knight.

A letter was addressed to Cooper by H.C. Knight's solicitors (Whitakers and Wool-bert) dated 30 December 1861, to which there was no reply.

Counsel was asked to advise whether an action for trespass would lie against Cooper and Bench or either of them, and whether such action would be better brought in the name of H.C. Knight or of the tenant.

Opinion

An action would lie at the tenant's suit against either Cooper or Bench, or both. Mr. Knight should not be plaintiff.

Signed: W.O. Edge, Temple, 25 January 1862.

67a. [January 1862]

Draft of case only.

68.   7 December 1869

Copy of referee's award in the causes Andrews v. Knight and Knight v. Andrews.

The referee found that, in addition to the £61 paid into court by the defendant (H.C. Knight) in the first cause, a further sum of £30.0s.11d. was due from the defendant to the plaintiff. In the second cause he found for the defendant (Andrews) on all issues.

Each of the parties should pay his own costs as to the reference, and the Rev. H.C. Knight should pay two thirds and John Andrews one third of the costs of the award.

Award dated 7 December 1869, and sent with a covering letter dated 14 December 1869 from John Lane solr. at Stratford-on-Avon to the Rev. H.C. Knight, Heathlands, Malvern Wells.

Estate papers

Rentals and miscellaneous accounts

70.   7 July 1857

Rental of the estates of the Rev. H.C. Knight in the parish of Wootton Wawen, co. Warwick.   Half a year's rent due at Lady Day 1857.   Received this 7 July 1857 by me, Edw: Cooper.

Comprises:		
	Moat House & Great Hallend farms & cottages	463 acres
	[Henley] farmhouse, offices &c.	165
	Chapel House & land	20
	Spur inn, garden &c.	—
	Cottage rents, area not specified	
	Mockley &c. woods	65
		713 acres

Gross rental: £427.15s.6d.   Nett sum received (less deductions and arrears): £347.8s.8d. Ullenhall tithe rentcharges and garden rents to follow.

71.   4 January 1859

Rental of the estates of the Rev. H.C. Knight in the parish of Wootton Wawen, co. Warwick.   Half a year's rent and one year's tithe rentcharge due at Michaelmas 1858.   Received this 4 January 1859 by me, Edw: Cooper.

Moat House farm (248 acres) and Great Hallend farm (215 acres) now in separate holdings.

Gross rental: £572.14s.10d.   Nett sum received: £380.19s.9d.

72.   28 March 1853

Memorandum of outgoings on E. Cooper's farm, allotment gardens and old house in Henley.

Includes the following:

> Land tax on Fosters
> Property tax on allotments and old house
> To the poor of Warwick
> Chief rents to Captain Musgrave
> To the poor of Henley on Tenter closes
> To the poor of Henley on Wad close
> [Poor] rate on allotments and old house
> Highway rate
> Church rate

Total outgoings: £13.4s.0d.

Signed: Edw: Cooper, 28 March 1853.

73.   1868

Memorandum of tithe rentcharge [of the Rev. H.C. Knight at Ullenhall] showing name of tenant, landowner, acreage, apportionment, and amount collected, or to be collected, in 1868.

Endorsed: Tithe rent charge for 1868, 1872, 1874.

74.   April 1878 - March 1879

Monthly accounts for Fosters farm and Moat House farm as follows:

Fosters farm (printed heading)   April-August 1878
Moat House farm (altered in MS)   September 1878-February 1879
Moat House farm (MS heading)   March 1879

Land tax certificates

75.   9 May 1799

Certificate of registration in the Land-Tax Register-Office, no. 14,774, of contract with Robert Knight esq. for redemption by him of land tax of £2.4s.8d. charged on lands in Henley-in-Arden. Dated 9 May 1799.

Pasted on verso of first membrane of no. 2 above.

76.   23 March 1813

Certificate of two of the land-tax commissioners that they had contracted with Robert Knight of Barrells esq. for the redemption by him of £12.16s.2d. land tax charged on
(1)   Farmhouse and c. 89 acres of land in Henley-in-Arden in the parish of Wootton Wawen, theretofore the property of Mrs. [blank] Baker, Thomas Handy and others and then in the occupation of James Thomas;
(2)   Farmhouse and c. 86 acres of land called the Heath in Ullenhall in Wootton Wawen then in the occupation of Francis Heming, late the property of John Burman esq. and formerly in the occupation of Joseph Court;
(3)   Public house and premises in Ullenhall then in the occupation of Mary Greaves;
(4)   Messuage then divided into two tenements with the perry mill orchard and c. 3 acres of land in Ullenhall, formerly the property of Mr. Pitts, late in the occupation of Joseph Ward and then of siad Joseph Ward and Elizabeth Moore;
(5)   Messuage then lately divided into two tenements with garden and c. 4 acres of land in Ullenhall in the occupation of Joseph Heming, formerly property of Mrs. Chamberlain and in the occupation of Isaac Bolton.

With certificate of two of the commissioners of land-tax for the Hundred of Barlichway as to the amounts charged, dated 26 March 1813, attached; also certificate of registration in the Land-tax Register-Office, no. 106,102 dated 17 April 1813.

Endorsed: Purchase No. [16 altered to] 17 & others.

77.   23 May 1814

Certificate of two of the land-tax commissioners that they had contracted with Robert Knight of 44 Grosvenor Square co. Middx. esq. for the redemption by him of 4s. land tax charged on a messuage or cottage with garden and small close of land in Ullenhall lately purchased of Mr. John Green and then or late in the occupation of William Smith.

From George Coppage to Robert Knight.   1830.
Taking down the Mausoleum in Barrells Park.

1830. Dec 24. Myself 1½ days at 3/4d per day	5 - 0
George Smith 1½ days at 1/8d	2 - 6
1831. Jan 1. Myself 5½ days at 3/4d	18 - 4
Labourer 11 days at 1/8d	18 - 4
12,400 bricks cleaned at 2/6d per 1,000	£1 - 11 - 0
Similar items amount to	£19 - 11 - 0

	£23 - 6 - 0

Robert Knight and his wife Frances separated after 17 years of marriage. They had three children, a son Henry who died while still an infant and two daughters Frances and Georgiana Knight.   There was another son, the Rev. Henry Charles Knight but Robert Knight denied being his father.   In 1825 Robert Knight owing to his family troubles moved away from Barrells and pulled down farm buildings and generally let the house and grounds deteriorate so that there would be little of value for Rev. Knight to inherit.   When he died in 1855 the estate was sold and to avoid the heavy legal costs involved Rev. H.C. Knight and Robert Knights nephew Charles Raleigh Knight agreed to divide the proceeds of the property.

The Barrells Estate was sold in London on June 20th, 1856 and was bought by Mr William Newton, a Birmingham Merchant, who proceeded to improve the property.   He removed the portico and built new kitchens and stables but was not there long enough to really see the results of his endeavours.   He died in Nov 1862 and was succeeded by his son Mr Thomas Henry Goodwin Newton, who made many more improvements to the house and grounds.   There was a large walled kitchen garden with its own well, and an avenue of laburnum trees planted to the lodge gates. A great many village people worked for Mr Newton and there is no doubt that he brought most benefits to the village with the building projects he undertook.

Sale Notices of Barrells Estate 1856.

IN THE COUNTIES OF WARWICK AND WORCESTER.

Particulars

THE BARRELS ESTATE,

A VALUABLE AND IMPORTANT

FREEHOLD PROPERTY,

Situate in the Parishes of Wootton Wawen, Studley, Tanworth, and Beaudesert,

IN THE COUNTIES OF WARWICK AND WORCESTER,

CLOSE TO THE TOWN OF HENLEY-IN-ARDEN,

About Eight miles from Stratford-on-Avon, Ten miles from Warwick, Eleven from Leamington, Fourteen from Birmingham, Fourteen from Bromsgrove, and within Four and a-half hours' journey of London ; comprising

THE BARRELS MANSION HOUSE,

Placed in a nicely timbered Park, with

THE MANORS OF OLDBERROW, ULLENHALL, FORDHALL, AND ASPLEIGH ;

SEVERAL

Farmhouses, Farm Buildings, Numerous Cottages, and Enclosures of Arable, Meadow, Pasture, and Woodland,

THE WHOLE CONTAINING

ABOUT THREE THOUSAND AND FORTY ACRES,

AND PART OF THE

IMPROPRIATE TITHE RENTCHARGE FOR THE TOWNSHIP OF ULLENHALL.

Which will be Sold by Auction,

BY MESSRS.

NORTON, HOGGART, AND TRIST,

AT THE AUCTION MART, LONDON,

On FRIDAY, JUNE 20TH, 1856, AT TWELVE O'CLOCK,

IN 16 LOTS,

Unless the whole should be previously disposed of in One Lot by Private Contract, of which due notice will be given.

May be viewed by application to Mr. COOPER, *the resident Agent ; and Particulars had at the* SWAN INN, *Henley-in-Arden ; the* HEN AND CHICKENS, *Birmingham ; the principal Inns in Warwick, Leamington, and Stratford ; of Messrs.* BIRCHAM, DALRYMPLE, AND DRAKE, *46, Parliament Street, Westminster ; Messrs.* PARKE AND POLLOCK, *63, Lincoln's Inn Fields ;* E. T. WHITAKER, Esq., *12, Lincoln's Inn Fields ; of Messrs.* DENTON AND DRAKE, *Surveyors, 52, Parliament Street, Westminster ; at the* MART, *and of Messrs.* NORTON, HOGGART, AND TRIST, *62, Old Broad Street, Royal Exchange.*

Metchim and Burt, Printers and Lithographers, 6 and 20, Parliament Street, Westminster.

LOT 12.

A VALUABLE FREEHOLD PROPERTY,

KNOWN AS THE SWAN INN,

Situate in the Parish of Wootton Wawen, in the centre of the Town of Henley-in-Arden,

CONTAINING NUMEROUS

BEDROOMS, PARLOURS, COMMERCIAL ROOM, BAR, BAR-PARLOUR, KITCHEN AND OFFICES, GOOD CELLARS, WITH GARDEN, BOWLING GREEN, AND PADDOCK,

The whole containing

Five Acres, One Rood, and Twenty-six Perches,

Lying as follows—

								A.	R.	P.
1	Swan Premises and Yard	...	...	...	...			0	1	28
2	Croft	...	...	...	...	Pasture	...	1	1	39
3	Bowling Green	...	...	...	...	Ditto	...	0	1	22
4	Little Bowling Green Close	...	...	...	Ditto	...	3	0	17
							A.	5	1	26

In the occupation of Mr. ROBERT OVERBURY.

This Lot is free from Land-tax, but subject to a Chief-rent of 6s. 6½d. payable to the Lord of the Manor of Henley.

LOT 13.

A FREEHOLD RESIDENCE,

Situate in the Town of Henley-in-Arden,

And formerly Occupied by the late Mr. KNIGHT,

WITH YARD, BUILDINGS, ORCHARD, AND PADDOCK IN THE REAR, COTTAGE, AND AGENCY OFFICES,

The whole containing

Eight Acres, Three Roods, and Twenty-three Perches,

Lying as follows—

									A.	R.	P.
1	Offices, Yard, &c.	...	...	...	...	...	...	...	0	2	10
2	Orchard	...	...	...	...	...	...	...	0	2	13
3	Home Close	...	...	...	...	...	...	...	2	3	29
4	Far Close	...	...	...	...	...	...	...	4	3	5
5	Slip at Henley	...	...	...	...	...	...	...	0	0	6
								A.	8	3	23

This Lot is free from Land Tax, but is subject to Chief-rents amounting to 2s. 1d. payable to the Lord of the Manor of Henley, and 1s. 6d. a year payable to the Poor of Warwick.

No. 4 is in the occupation of Mr. E. COOPER, and the Slip at Henley of Mr. G. Blower ; the other part is in hand.

LOT 14.

THE SPUR INN, A VALUABLE FREEHOLD PUBLIC HOUSE,

Situate in the Parish of Wootton Wawen, in the Village of Ullenhall,

CONTAINING

FIVE BEDROOMS, BAR-PARLOUR, KITCHEN, BREWHOUSE AND CELLARS, STABLING,
AND OFFICES OPPOSITE, ALSO A COTTAGE AND GARDEN.

The whole containing

One Rood and Eleven Perches,

Lying as follows—

						A.	R.	P.
196	Spur Inn, Stable, and Garden	...	...	...	...	0	0	37
497a	Cottage and Garden	...	...	...	...	0	0	14
					A.	0	1	11

In the occupation of Mr. ROBERT TATHAM. (This Lot is free from Land-tax).

LOT 15.

FOUR FREEHOLD COTTAGES AND GARDENS,

Situate in the Village of Ullenhall,

Nos. 494, 493, 495, and 496a, the whole containing

Two Roods and Twenty-three Perches,

In the occupation of JOHNS, BROWN, PUGH, and GEE,

LOT 16.

A VALUABLE FREEHOLD RENTCHARGE,

IN LIEU OF TITHES,

Commuted at £65 13s. per Annum,

AND EXTENDING OVER ABOUT FOUR HUNDRED AND TWENTY-FIVE ACRES OF LAND,

In the Parish of Ullenhall.

This Lot will be sold subject to the payment of a charge of £9 5s. 4d. per annum to the Vicar of Wootton Wawen, and to
£6 per annum to the Minister of Bewley.

Barrells Hall showing servants quarters to the right.

Barrells Hall - the opposite side.

Some of the outdoor workforce at Barrells Hall.

A celebration at Barrells Hall.

The Lodge at the entrance to Barrells Hall from the Henley Road.

August 20th 1886. Horticultural Show

On Tuesday last a show of vegetables, fruit and flowers was held at Barrells Park, kindly lent by Mr T.H. Newton. This was the second annual exhibition of the kind held at Ullenhall and was a great success. The weather was favourable and a large number of visitors from Ullenhall, Henley and surrounding parishes inspected the exhibits, which were staged in a suitable marqee. The exhibition was divided into 2 classes, one being open to cottagers residing in Ullenhall and other parishes and the other for amateurs. In the cottagers class the entries were numerous and the quality of exhibits very fine. The exhibits of the amateurs were not numerous and in point of quality were far inferior to those shown by the cottagers. In this class the prize takers included several competitors from Henley.

Mr T. Newton exhibited a fine collection of fruit including peaches, nectarines and grapes, also Mr Joseph Smith of Henley and Mr J .W. Cockle of Ullenhall. An honourary exhibitor showed some excellent fruit and vegetables. In the evening the prizes were distributed by Mrs Newton. At the conclusion of the ceremony hearty cheers were given to Mr & Mrs Newton for endeavouring to promote the success of the show. An excellent band from Redditch performed a selection of music during the afternoon and in the evening a large number of persons took part in dancing.

Report of Dec 10th 1887.

The death was reported on Dec 1st 1887 of the Rev. H.C. Knight after a long illness. Some years ago he sold Barrells (which had been in the Knight family for more than 300 years) to Mr Newton the father of our present High Sherriff. Mr Knight became a widower in 1884 and leaves a family of four daughters.

In 1887 Mr T.H.G. Newton became High Sherriff of Warwickshire and during his lifetime at Barrells Hall a considerable amount of entertaining was done to celebrate some occasion or another.

On Jan 8th 1887 Mr Newton of Barrells Park entertained to dinner one hundred and fifty men with their wives from the immediate neighbourhood of Ullenhall and Oldberrow who were known to be adherents to the Conservative cause. After the cloth had been removed, addresses were given by Rev. M. West, T. Newton and F. Townsend M.P. Several of the company rendered songs at intervals, amongst them being Mrs F. Townsend who sang 'Rule Brittania'. The brass band from Henley-in-Arden were in attendance and enlivened the proceedings by playing several of their selections. The company broke up soon after 10 o'clock after having thoroughly enjoyed themselves.

Report of 10th June 1887.

On Monday last this pretty little village was quite en Fete, the occasion being the usual monthly visit of the Henley Brass Band, who by the kind permission of Miss Newton will give a public rehearsal on the first Monday in every month at the new Coffee House. Owing to the fine weather the performance took place out of doors and attracted a large number of the inhabitants to the spot, which, coupled with the cheerful ringing of the church bells, put one in mind of a jubilee in advance.

June 25th. 1887. Jubilee

Inhabitants of Ullenhall and Oldberrow met at the Vicarage gates and sang the National Anthem, followed by a service in the church taken by Rev. West. There was also a service at Oldberrow taken by Rev. S. Peshall. The two parishes joined at Barrells. Canvas was erected to protect people from the sun. Dinner was of roast beef and other joints, rabbit pies, ham, plum puddings etc. Rev. West presided in absence of the High Sherriff who was taking part in the ceremony at Westminster Abbey. About 325 persons sat down to dinner. Rev. West proposed 'The Queen' and the toast was heartily received and the National Anthem sung.

Mrs Newton presented two medals gained by school children in the High Sherriff's competition to Gilbert Docker and Ellen Partington. A programme of sports was carried out during the rest of the day and the Victoria Brass Band from Redditch played music. The day ended with a bonfire of 30 loads of brushwood kindled on Crowley's Hill.

July 6th 1893

The marriage day of the Duke of York and Princess May of Teck was celebrated in Ullenhall by a high tea and evening in the Barrell's grounds, to which Mr Newton invited all the inhabitants of Ullenhall, Aspley and Oldberrow. After tea Mr Newton proposed the Royal Toast and said that this was the first occasion on which the son of one who was still Prince of Wales had been married. The Vicar proposed and Mr Wilkes seconded a vote of thanks to Mr Newton. A committee of which Mr Wilkes was secretary raised about £7 and arranged a list of twenty races, tugs of war and jumping contests for the men, women, boys and girls of the villages, which called forth numerous competitors. Mrs Newton distributed the prizes. The Redditch band again supplied the music. Fireworks concluded a very satisfactory celebration of the Royal Marriage.

July 7th 1893

The children of the parishes were invited by Mr Newton to commemorate the wedding of the previous day. About 125 in all were present, of whom Ullenhall School contributed 77. Tea at 4-30 was succeeded by various sports and games.. Miss N. Newton distributed the prizes and also presented medals to the senior children. Fireworks again successfully closed the day.

Mr Thomas Newton died in 1907 and the following is taken from his obituary notice in the Stratford Herald.

Deceased was the eldest son of the late Mr William Newton of Whateley Hall, Castle Bromwich and Barrells, Warwickshire and was born in 1836. He was educated at St. John's College, Cambridge where he graduated B.A. in 1858 and M.A. in 1861. On leaving University he studied for the bar. He was a member of the Middle Temple, but can scarcely be said to have practised as a barrister for shortly after he was called to the bar his father died and the life of Mr Newton became that of a country gentleman. He was a magistrate for the county of Warwick and became chairman of the Henley-in-Arden petty sessional division. In 1887 Jubilee year he was High Sherriff of the county and in that capacity was present in Birmingham in March when her Majesty the Queen came to lay the foundation stone of the new General Hospital. Mr Newton was a donor to the building fund of the institution. He formerly owned the large block of buildings bounded by New Street, Hill Street, Pinfold Street and the railway in Navigation Street, which some years ago was acquired and cleared by the Government to provide a site for the new Post Office. He was formerly a director of the Birmingham Trust (Ltd) and for many years a member of the Theatre Royal Company, joining the directorate when that property became vested with the Theatre Royal Estate Company. Mr Newton's principal residence was Barrells Hall formerly the residence of the Earls of Catherlough. It is in this neighbourhood that the best epitaph of his life-work lies. He would never discharge an old or inefficient man and was greatly adverse to any reduction in their wages when by reason of age or infirmity their work suffered by comparison.

He took a lively interest in the administration of local affairs and was a staunch churchman. In conjunction with his sisters and brothers he erected in 1875 at a cost of £5,000 a church as a memorial to their parents. The following year Mr Newton built the public elementary school (mixed) to accommodate 86 children. In politics he was a Conservative holding the position of chairman of the Henley-in-Arden polling district. Mr Newton shared with his brother, the Rev. Canon Newton the possession of Glencripesdale and Laudale, Argyllshire, a fine estate of 25,000 acres. Mr Newton was married three times, in 1861 he married a daughter of Mr W. Berrow, when she died he married again in 1865 and three sons and six daughters were born. Mrs Newton died in 1894 and in January 1898 Mr Newton married for the third time.

The internment took place in the family vault at the Old Chapel. The coffin was borne on a wheeled bier from the Hall to the old churchyard by four of the servants W. Pottell, F. Bullock, F. Baylis and French. The mourners were Mrs Newton (widow) Mr Hugh Newton, Mr Mark Newton, Mr H.W.G. Newton (sons), Miss Newton, Miss H.C. Newton, Miss E.M. Newton, Miss M.R. Newton, Miss J.R. Newton, Miss O.M. Newton (daughters), the Rev. Canon Newton (brother). Daughters-in-law were also present, neices and local dignitaries. Many local village people attended and flowers were sent from the cottagers and school-children at Ullenhall.

WARWICKSHIRE.

Final Sale to close the Estate of the late Hugh G. Newton, Esq.

➤◦◦◦◄

IN 26 LOTS.

THE REMAINING PARTS OF THE HIGHLY IMPORTANT AND VALUABLE

FREEHOLD ESTATE

(a very small portion being leasehold for nearly 1,700 years)

SITUATE IN PARISHES OF

Wootton Wawen, Henley-in-Arden, Morton Bagot and Oldberrow

About 14 miles from Birmingham and 2½ from Henley-in-Arden (G.W R.),

KNOWN AS

The Barrells Estate

COMPRISING THE

MANSION HOUSE, STABLING. GROUNDS and LODGE;

OLDBERROW COURT FARM, about 425 acres

(One of the finest Farms in the Midlands);

PARK BARN FARM, the OLD BUNGALOW, the "WINGED SPUR" INN,
the VILLAGE INSTITUTE, the VILLAGE SCHOOL HOUSE, a number of
COTTAGES, SPORTING WOODLANDS, COVERTS and PLANTATIONS,
ALLOTMENTS and FIELDS OF ACCOMMODATION LAND,
In and around Ullenhall and Henley-in-Arden. ALSO THE

Advowson and Perpetual Presentation of the Living of Ullenhall,

And the Lordship of the Manors of Ullenhall, Oldberrow and Aspley.

AREA ABOUT

740 ACRES

About 572 acres of which is in hand, and Possession will be given on Completion.

TO BE SOLD BY AUCTION, BY MESSRS.

LUDLOW, BRISCOE & HUGHES

At The Grand Hotel, Birmingham,

On Thursday, October the 23rd, 1924,

AT 4 P.M.

In 26 Lots, to suit all classes of purchasers.

➤◦◦◦◄

Vendors' Solicitors:
Messrs. ROWLEY, CHATWIN & EMERSON, 22, Church Street, Birmingham.

Auctioneers' Offices:
19, Temple Street, Birmingham.   Telephone, Central 537.   Telegrams, "Appraise."

After Mr T. Newton's death his son Mr Hugh Newton succeeded to the estate, but died suddenly in 1924.

Jack E. Brown, grandson of the blacksmith W.W. Clayton at Barrells Hall
27th February 1902, aged 11 years.

Stratford Herald, Friday July 4th 1924.

We regret to announce the death of Mr H.G. Newton of Barrell's Hall which occurred suddenly, following a heart attack on Thurs. of last week. The funeral took place at the Old Church on Tuesday. The officiating clergy were Revs. Canon Eagles, W.F. Pelton and J.P.L. Amos (brother-in-law of deceased). The chief mourners were Mrs H.G. Newton (widow), Messrs Richard and Hugh Newton (sons). Deaconess Maud Newton, Mrs Amos, Miss Newton and Mrs Headlam (sisters). Lieut. Commander M.G. Newton and Mr H.W.G. Newton (brothers). Many relations and friends were present and there was a large number of floral tributes. Mr F. Organ was in charge of the funeral arrangements.

Sale notice of West Lodge - Ullenhall.

LOT 4.

CHURCH ROAD, ULLENHALL.

THE DELIGHTFUL

Small Freehold Bungalow

formerly the West Lodge to Barrells Park. The House is black and white with thatched roof and a charming verandah in front, and contains a Living Hall fitted with range and cupboard, Pantry, Larder, and Scullery, and two Bedrooms; also Coal House, lean-to Shed, Outoffices and well, together with capital Garden.

There is sufficient land with this Lot for extending the existing Garden, forming tennis court, or for poultry keeping, the area being about acres 1.239 or

1a. 0r. 38p.

let to Mr. G. A. Cummins as annual tenant, Christmas entry, at the nominal rental of £4 0s. 0d. per annum. The grass land, part of No. 429, being in hand.

Timber, £5 0s. 0d.

REMARKS.—This Lot has a road frontage of about 100 yards, and has a splendid view to the South over Barrells Park. Included in the area is the magnificent old oak known as The Ullenhall Oak, one of the few remaining giant trees of the Ancient Forest of Arden.

NOTE.—*The Purchaser of Lot 4 shall forthwith erect and for ever thereafter maintain a good and sufficient fence where marked T on plan.*

———————— >◦◇◦< ————————

Following Mr Hugh Newton's death the Barrell's Estate which comprised a good part of the village properties was sold on Oct 23rd 1924. The total amount realised was £26,520. The prices of the respective lots are as follows: Barrell's Hall and Park £3,850, advowson of Ullenhall manorial rights £210, Park Barn Farm £2,600, the Bungalow £530, Oldberrow Court Farm £11,250, meadow land near Nutlands £260, old turf and arable land near Hunger Hill £295, pasture, Cadborough Bridge £210, pasture Chesters Green £860, sporting property near Out Hill £650, pasture land and woodland £490, Chesters Green Cottages £330, pasture land and road strips £95, gravel pit and rough ground £55, Winged Spur Inn £1,650, Smithy and garden £65, Institute and Cafe £565, building site £65, two cottages and gardens £340, two ditto and ditto £315, single cottage £295, School House and garden £450, allotments £180, Brickyard cottage £290, arable land Henley-in-Arden £360, meadow land £260.

However Barrells Hall and Oldberrow Court Farm were put up for re-sale on April 23rd 1925, with Barrells Hall being bought by Mr J.W. Marsh. Oldberrow Court Farm was sold again on Thursday July 16th 1931.

WARWICKSHIRE.

BARRELLS PARK

Near Henley-in-Arden, 14½ miles from Birmingham.

RE-SALE OF AN AREA OF ABOUT

542 ACRES

Divided into 13 most Interesting and Attractive Lots,

COMPRISING THE

Mansion House, known as Barrells Hall,

With Stabling, Lodge, Fish Ponds, and Part of the Park.

Area, about **50** Acres.

OLDBERROW COURT FARM,

One of the Best-known AGRICULTURAL and SPORTING PROPERTIES in the Midlands, with Old-fashioned HOMESTEAD and Extensive Modern FARM BUILDINGS. Area, about **285** Acres; and

11 other Lots of Fine Grazing Parklike Land

In all, about **207** Acres, being part of the ANCIENT PARK, having amble Shade and Water, three Lots having nearly-new DUTCH BARNS and BUILDINGS thereon, and all have long frontages to main roads. The whole Estate being **FREEHOLD,** with the exception of about 7 acres, which is Leasehold for over 1,500 Years and free from Ground Rent.

REMARKS.—This Sale affords the opportunity to a buyer of acquiring a fine Country House at almost a break-up price, also a first-class Farm, and to small capitalists and investors of possessing beautiful Parkland of the highest quality for Small Holdings, Dairying, Poultry Farming, or for the erection of moderate sized Country Houses, for which there are many unique Sites. With the exception of 17 acres, Possession can be had on Completion.

MESSRS. LUDLOW, BRISCOE & HUGHES

IN CONJUNCTION WITH

MESSRS. BARBER & SON

WILL SELL THE ABOVE BY AUCTION,

At the GRAND HOTEL, BIRMINGHAM,

On THURSDAY, APRIL 23rd, 1925,

At **3-0** p.m., unless Sold previously by Private Contract.

Particulars and Plans may be obtained at the Offices of Messrs. BARBER AND SON, Auctioneers, 1, Church Street, Wellington, Salop; and Messrs. LUDLOW, BRISCOE, & HUGHES, 19, Temple Street, Birmingham.
Telephone Central 537. Telegrams, "Appraise, Birmingham."

Solicitors: Messrs. CHRISTOPHERS & LODDER, Henley-in-Arden.

Sarah Palmer, daughter of Charlie Palmer who worked on Barrells Estate. She is wearing one of the capes given to girls by the Newton family. The boys were given woollen jerseys.

The Old Thatched Lodge - Ullenhall.

William Tomlin, tenant of Chapel Farm.

LOT 18.

A Capital Freehold Building Site

adjoining Lot 17, comprising part of an old Garden facing the Village Street and a small Paddock at the back, the whole containing an area of about acres .314 or

0a. 1r. 10p.

The front Garden is partly in the occupation of the Tenants of Lots 17 and 19, and the piece of Grass Land at the back is in the occupation of Mr. R. Franklin, as annual Tenant, Michaelmas entry, at the apportioned rent of 4/- per annum.

REMARKS.—*This Lot is most admirably adapted for the erection of a small Bungalow or Cottage. There is a water supply in the main street, to which it has a frontage of about 30 yards.*

NOTE.—*The Purchaser of Lot 18 will have to erect and for ever hereafter maintain a good and sufficient fence where marked T on Plan.*

LOT 19.

Two Brick and Tile Freehold Cottages,

nearly opposite the War Memorial in Ullenhall Village, in the occupation of Joseph Tomlin at a rental of £5 8s. 0d. per annum payable half-yearly, and J. Cox at a rental of £5 15s. 0d. per annum payable half-yearly.

Each House contains Kitchen, Living Room, two Bedrooms, also Outoffices and Gardens, and a small Shop let to Miss Crook at 1s. per week on a weekly tenancy, together with a piece of Old Turf Land at the back thereof, in the occupation of Mr. R. Franklin as annual Tenant, Michaelmas entry, at the apportioned rent of 4s. per annum. Area, about acres .372 or

0a. 1r. 19p.

NOTE.—*The Purchaser of this Lot will have to erect and for ever hereafter maintain a good and sufficient fence where marked T on plan.*

REMARKS.—*These are two useful Cottages, and they have an additional attraction in the piece of Old Turf Land at the back.*

Two Freehold Brick and Tile Cottages,

containing Kitchen, Scullery, two Bedrooms, Outoffices, and Gardens. Let to Robert Wyatt at a rental of £4 10s. 0d. per annum annual tenancy, Michaelmas entry, and Miss Steely at a rent of £4 10s. 0d. per annum annual tenancy, Michaelmas entry, Tenants paying all rates and taxes except water rate.

The Stable between the two Cottages is in the occupation of Mr. William Walker, with Lot 15, at the apportioned rent of 10/- per annum, annual tenancy, Michaelmas entry, Tenant paying all rates and taxes; also a piece of old Turf Land at the back thereof, let to Mr. R. Franklin as annual Tenant, Michaelmas entry. Apportioned rent 4s. per annum. Area about acres .387 or

0a. 1r. 22p.

NOTE.—*This is a capital site in the centre of the Village, and there is room for the erection of one or more Cottages on the spare land.*

The Purchaser of this Lot shall forthwith erect and for ever after maintain a good and sufficient fence, where marked T on plan.

There is a Tithe of 4/6 (commuted) on Lots 17 to 20 inclusive.

THE DOUBLE-FRONTED

Freehold Brick and Tile Cottage,

opposite the " Winged Spur " Public House, containing Living Room, Kitchen, Scullery, two Bedrooms, Garden, and Outoffices, also Garden and small piece of Old Turf Land at the back, the whole containing an area of about acres .179 or

0a. 0r. 29p.

Part of the Garden is in the occupation of Mr. William Walker, with Lot 15, at the apportioned rent of 10s. per annum annual tenancy, Michaelmas entry. The Cottage is in hand.

REMARKS.—*With a small expenditure this Dwelling House could be made into a useful Week-end Cottage.*

THE VERY PLEASANT

Brick and Tile Freehold Cottage Residence

known as

"THE SCHOOL HOUSE,"

adjoining the Village Schools, containing Entrance Hall, Sitting Room, and Parlour, Kitchen, Pantry, Yard, and Outoffices; three Bedrooms, Clothes Closet, and large and productive Garden, with outside W.C.   Area, about acres .230 or

0a. 0r. 37p.

The Cottage is let to the Warwickshire Education Committee, with part of the Garden, at a rent of £12 0s. 0d. per annum annual tenancy, Ladyday entry, Tenant paying rates and taxes.

REMARKS.—*This Cottage was built by the late Mr. Newton's father in the year 1876, at the same time as the Schools, and is in every way a very desirable small Country Residence.*

———————————— >◦◦◦< ————————————

LOT 22.

The Important Freehold Property,

now let as ALLOTMENTS, near to the Village of Ullenhall, being No. 363 Ordnance Survey, and containing an area of acres 5.338, or about

5a. 1r. 14p.,

let to various Tenants at 10/- per allotment, and producing a rental, when fully let, of £11 per annum, Landlord paying rates and taxes.

REMARKS.—*This land is eminently suited for market gardening and fruit and vegetable growing. It is in an elevated position, and a capital site for the erection of Cottages by the County Authorities, with ample space for Gardens attached thereto, and has a road frontage of nearly a quarter of a mile.*

LOT 16

The Freehold Business Premises,

built of brick and tile, situated in the Village of Ullenhall, adjoining Lot 17, comprising the RETAIL SHOP, with comfortable dwelling house attached thereto, adjoining which is a bakehouse, cart shed, stable, loft, and other erections, also a large garden opposite, the whole being in the occupation of Mr. Tatnall, Grocer and Draper, as a quarterly tenant, paying rates; together with a Piece of good MEADOW LAND, the whole containing an area of about

1a. 2r. 16p.

as set forth in the following Schedule.

SCHEDULE OF LANDS COMPRISED IN LOT 16,

IN THE PARISH OF WOOTTON WAWEN, County of Warwick.

Ord. No.	Description.	Area. Acres.	Tenant.	Rental.	Remarks.
				£ s. d.	
Pt. 334	Shop and Dwelling House	.037	Mr. Wm. H. Tatnall	13 0 0	Quarterly tenant
Pt. 347	Garden	.094			
Pt. 347	Paddock	1.469	Mr. C. Friend	1 0 0	Annual tenancy Ladyday entry
	Acres	1.600		£14 0 0	Apportioned rent

Timber, £

Apportioned Tithe, 1s. 0d.

REMARKS.—This is a useful property, in good order, low rented, and should appeal to the small investor. Tap water is laid on.

Two Old-fashioned Dwelling Houses

adjoining "Rose Cottage" in Ullenhall Village. One built of brick and tile, containing kitchen, scullery, dairy, outoffices, and three bedrooms, together with a good garden and pigsty; the other is larger and is double-fronted, built of brick, with slate roof, containing hall entrance, sitting room, kitchen, scullery, larder, cellar, outoffices, and three bedrooms, also a good garden and a Paddock of OLD TURF LAND at the back, in which is a wind engine belonging to the Stratford-on-Avon Rural District Council; the whole containing an area of about

oa. 3r. 31p.,

as set forth in the following Schedule.

SCHEDULE OF LANDS COMPRISED IN LOT 18,

IN THE PARISH OF WOOTTON WAWEN, County of Warwick.

Ord. No.	Description.	Area. Acres.	Tenant.	Rental.	Remarks.
				£ s. d.	
Pt. 334	Cottage and Garden		Mr. F. J. Tomlin	5 8 0	Quarterly tenancy Landlord paying rates and taxes
Pt. 334	Dwelling House and Garden	.945	Mr. C. Friend	3 0 0	Let with Farm Annual tenancy Ladyday entry Apportioned rent
Pt. 333	Paddock		Mr. H. Gould	0 15 0	Annual tenancy Ladyday entry Apportioned rent
	Acres	.945		£9 3 0	

Timber, £

REMARKS.—This Lot is capable, at a small expense, of being converted into a comfortable small Country House, and the piece of old Turf Land is most useful as an orchard or for poultry keeping. It is sold with the right-of-way over Lot 13, in common with the owner of Lot 17, and subject to a right-of-way to Lot 17, as shown on Plan, and the Wind Engine and Well are leased to the Stratford-on-Avon Rural District Council for 99 years, from March 25th, 1919, together with a right-of-way thereto.

44

The Ullenhall Estate which was entailed to Rev. H.C. Knight was sold on July 10th 1919. This comprised Hall End Farm, Moat House Farm, Blunts Green Farm, Chapel Farm and numerous attractive building sites etc.

By direction of the Trustees of the late Rev. H. C. Knight.

WARWICKSHIRE.

THE

ULLENHALL ESTATE.

Particulars, Photographs and Plan of a Valuable and Important

FREEHOLD PROPERTY

of about 492 acres,

Situate near HENLEY-IN-ARDEN, in the PARISH OF WOOTTON WAWEN, about 14 miles from Birmingham, 8 miles from Stratford-on-Avon and 5 miles from Redditch.

The North Warwickshire line of the Great Western Railway runs through the Estate, and Danzey Green Station is within half a mile.

THE ESTATE COMPRISES:—

"HALL END FARM,"
166a. 3r. 14p.

"MOAT HOUSE FARM,"
130a. 3r. 12p.

"BLUNTS GREEN FARM,"
44a. 0r. 27p.

"CHAPEL FARM,"
53a. 3r. 32p.

and **Numerous Attractive Building Sites, Small Holdings, Cottages,** and **Valuable Woodland** (part of Hobditch Coppice); also

FREEHOLD PROPERTIES,

High Street, HENLEY-IN-ARDEN,

together with

TITHE RENT CHARGES

Of the annual commuted value of **£63 18s. 7d.**, receivable in 14 amounts.

EDWARDS, SON & BIGWOOD

WILL SELL THE ABOVE BY AUCTION, AT THE

GRAND HOTEL, COLMORE ROW, BIRMINGHAM,

On Thursday, July 10th, 1919,

At 3 p.m. precisely.

45

Moat House Farm.

In the early part of 1933 a terrible fire broke out at Barrells Hall. A report in the Birmingham Gazette of 25th April 1933 is headed:-

All day fire at Mansion. No occupants.

Damage estimated at thousands of pounds was caused by a fire which broke out early yesterday and raged for many hours at Barrells Hall, a well known Warwickshire mansion at Ullenhall.   Flames were noticed shortly after midnight and the Stratford fire brigade was summoned.   The rear part of the hall was burning fiercely when the firement arrived.   The brigade had an arduous time.   For more than 18 hours they were engaged in combating the flames before they were finally extinguished.   At 6.30 last night the firemen returned to the station with the knowledge that although the rear portion of the hall had been gutted they had saved the front part of the building.   They had to run hose from an adjacent lake to obtain a supply of water to cope with the outbreak, which after being overcome, caused trouble through bursting out afresh in the smouldering timbers.   At the time of the outbreak the spacious building was unoccupied.

Since that time the building has been crumbling away to an overgrown ruin, with little to show of the once imposing Mansion and beautiful grounds.   The stable block and coach house, a short distance from the main building remain in good condition and some lovely tall trees still stand.   Further into the grounds is the well preserved and well covered egg shaped ice house.

The Barrells Estate Before the Fire.

ULLENHALL PUDDING

No one has any memories of an Ullenhall Pudding, or the recipe, but it seems to have been special enough to be treated with reverence and eaten with great delight on special occasions. At one of the celebratory dinners at Barrells Hall an Ullenhall Pudding was served but no mention is made of any of the ingredients.

Another reference is made in this account from the Stratford Herald:-

Oct. 29 1886

On Tuesday last the High Bailiff Mr John Hannett assembled round him at the Bell Inn, Henley, a plentiful dinner of old English cheer. The remaining number of the first gathering of old men to celebrate his birthday, the present one being the eighty first. After the 'roast and boiled' were well disposed of, the usual celebrated 'Ullenhall Pudding' on one of the ancient Corporation dishes was placed on the table and speedily vanished from sight.

THE COFFEE HOUSE

The Coffee House was built in 1883 by the Newton family and housed the Village Club which had previously held meetings at Park Barn. The club was equipped by Miss Lizzie Newton and was open six days a week. Games such as bagatelle, chess, dominoes, draughts and cards were provided. A lending library was started and the clubroom was hired for whist drives, parties and dances. Cups of coffee and soft drinks were sold there. It is recorded in 1880 that 4,000 cups of coffee were sold.

Account from Stratford Herald April 23 1887

On Tuesday last a concert was held in the Coffee House, the proceeds to be devoted to that useful institution. The chair was taken by Rev. M. West, 160 being present. The schoolchildren recited 'Meddlesome Matty' and other poems at intervals. Miss Westfield sang 'Victoria', Charles Scragge sang 'Queen and Country', Harry Pugh sang 'Flower Gatherers' to mention a few renditions. Rev. West gave thanks to those who contributed to its success.

After the Barrells Estate was sold a Village Institute was formed at the Coffee House in 1927, more or less carrying on the previous activities.

Band of Hope Movement

Two of the Misses Newton lived at Heath Lodge and started Band of Hope meetings there. On Monday Dec 19th 1887 Members of the C. of

E. Temperance Society gave a concert in the schoolroom Miss Sumner played a Piano Solo "Chime again beautiful Bells". The Band of Hope children recited "Timothy Hubble" and sang 'Pulling hard against the stream'. Mr J. Bennett recited 'The geese and the cherries' and Mr W. Knight sang 'Until those footsteps come again' etc. The evening finished with the National Anthem.

Heath Lodge - Ullenhall

ULLENHALL VILLAGE INSTITUTE

Opened on Nov 26th 1927 by Major Bradbury for the village of the above. An enjoyable evening was spent with concert and whist drive.

The first General Meeting was held on Tuesday Nov 29th 1927. Major Bradbury was proposed for president with Mr Siddall Jones as Treasurer and Mr A.E. Morrall as Secretary.

A committee meeting was held on 2nd Dec 1927. Present were Mrs Pelton, Miss Richmond, Miss Steeley, Miss Pugh, Miss Barrett, Mr Barrett, Mr Wilkes, Mr Jones and Mr Alcott. The following rules were drawn up:-

1.   That the name be the Ullenhall Village Institute.
2.   Subscription 1/- per month for males, 6d per month for females and 3d per night for visitors.

3.   That there shall be no gambling.
4.   The club be open each weeknight 6 o'clock until 10 o'clock except Saturday when it shall be opened from 2 o'clock until 10 o'clock.
5.   Any member giving undesirable conduct shall be reported to the committee and liable to be expelled from the Institute.

Committee Meeting June 8th 1928.

It was proposed that as the Institute is in financial difficulties that the caretakers house be let at a rent of 10/- per week.
2.   That the rent of the Institute for May be paid to Mr Alcott.

Committee Meeting Sept 7th 1928.

A recommendation be made at the general meeting that the subscription be 1/- per month for both ladies and gentlemen.

Committee Meeting 7th Dec 1929.

It was proposed that the gentlemen should have a free supper about Xmas and it should be rabbit pie and cider.   The date was fixed for 27th Dec 1929.

Committee Meeting 7th Feb 1930.

An entertainment on the 15th Feb 1930 by the Ladies Amateur Dramatic Society.   Tickets 1/- and 1/6d reserved seats at 7.30 p.m.

Special Committee Meeting Oct 22nd 1930.

Secretary W. Robbins asked that committee members be protected to enable them to do their duty fearlessly.   If any member obstruct or interfere with a member of committee during or after duty, such member to be brought before full committee and fined if deemed necessary, and until such fine is paid the said member to be expelled from Clubroom.

Entertainment Committee Nov 26th 1930.

Moved by Miss Richmond and seconded by Mrs Tomlin that a Whist Drive and Dance be held on Dec at the usual price of 6d.

Moved by Mrs Tomlin and seconded by Mr L. Richmond that a Whist Drive and Dance (Fancy & Comic) be held on Dec 31st 1930.

Moved by Mrs Tomlin and seconded by Miss Richmond that a Rabbit and Beef supper be held on Jan 9th 1931 and a charge of 6d be made, only paid members to be eligible.

Committee Meeting Jan 2nd 1931.

Owing to the generosity of the President (Turkey, plum pudding, cider and lemonade) was to be provided for the Christmas Supper and Mrs Jones will give the mincepies.   The Vicar Mr Pelton be asked to be Guest for that night.

Committee Meeting Feb 6th 1931.

It was agreed to let the proposed Cricket Club have a room for a meeting for the sum of 1/- to cover fire and light cost.

Committee Meeting March 27th 1931.

The date of closing the Institute was then brought forward, it was moved by Mr Richards and seconded by Mr Wells that April 18th be the date.

Committee Meeting Feb 2nd 1932.

The Secretary reported that the Bagatelle Table had been sold.

Sixth General Meeting Oct 13th 1932.

Rev. Whittaker was elected President. The first Whist Drive to be held on October 26th, admission 6d and one every fortnight through the season.

Committee Meeting Oct 13th 1932.

It was decided to give prizes to the value of 2/6d first prize and 1/6d for second prize and charge 1½d for cakes, sandwiches, tea and coffee.

Committee Meeting Dec 8th 1932.

The Wireless Set was then discussed again and finally Miss Steeley offered 5/- for same and this was accepted.
The question of the proposed Village Hall was discussed.

Committee Meeting Jan 5th 1933.

The Committee are of the opinion that it is not expedient to amalgamate with the Women's Institute at the present juncture in the formation of a Village Hall. For the supper on Jan 14th the secretary was instructed to obtain ham, beef, pickles, bread rolls, mince pies, tea, coffee, milk and cigarettes and also to obtain the services of Mrs Jones for Community Singing.

Committee Meeting Feb 27th 1933.

Whist Drives were arranged for Feb 28th, March 15th and April 5th. The last named to be admission 1/- and at which better prizes were to be given. 2 First Prizes 8/-, 2 second prizes 5/-, 2 consolation prizes 2/-, Dancers Prizes 2/6d. The Dance this special night was arranged to be on till 1 o'clock. .

This seems to end the activities of the Village Institute with the building of the Village Hall then taking over the Whist Drives, dances and Women's Institute meetings. The Coffee House was then used by the Cadbury family to bring children out from Birmingham to the countryside. At this time it began to be called the 'Camp House'. The vicar Rev. W. Cooper was concerned at one stage with the clothing of the girls and borrowed scarves from the Vicarage to cover the girls heads in church.

The Coffee House and Institute, with the Vicarage in the background.

ULLENHALL SCHOOL

The first mention of a school of any sort in Ullenhall is a Free School which was held in the north-east corner of the Old Chapel. Six boys and two girls were registered there in 1798 with Thomas Astley as school master, being paid £4 per year. At some time a room in the charity cottages nearby was also used. Before Ullenhall school itself was built the school was held at Barrell's Hall with Miss Emily Carpenter as school-mistress.

In 1876 the village school and school house was built by Mr T.H.G. Newton. The schoolmistress in 1894 was Miss Elizabeth Yorke followed by Miss Hannah Crookes in 1908 assisted by Miss Mary Brown then Miss Albrighton. The pupils stayed at school until they were 14 years old. There were two rooms at the school, the smaller one for infants and the larger one for juniors, the lighting was by oil lamps and the only means of heating in wintertime was a fire place in each room. The fires were big open fires with black leaded surrounds and whitened hearths. Sometimes it was so cold that it was difficult to hold a pen. When the children in the front rows were warm enough they moved further back so that other children could move forward to thaw out. There was wood block flooring and a large coal place outside.

54

Miss Crookes, Rev. and Mrs West, Mary Brown teacher seated in front of Ullenhall School House.

Miss Crookes, Headmistress. Front row, fourth from left Nancy Tomlin, second row left Dorothy Taylor, third girl along is Flo Morgan.

Miss Albrighton with infants class. The winged spur is in the background. Middle of second row, Grace Neal with white bow of ribbon. Girl on the end with two white bows, Catherine Taylor.

Boys and girls in the 1920-30's were segregated in the playground by a wooden fence up the middle but later on this disappeared. Girls at that time would walk to Henley one day a week for cookery and laundry lessons, boys would work on the allotments. Girls did knitting and sewing at school and if they forgot to bring work to do they were given the task of darning Miss Albrighton's black stockings, of which she had a large supply.

The desks were made for two with seats that made a noisy clang every time the pupils stood up or sat down. There were two bucket toilets outside, one for the girls and the other for the teachers. The boys had red brick enclosures at the far end of the playground, largely open to the elements.

School outing near Bristol. At the back left is Mrs Mahoney next to Flo Lamb. Boy at front left is Jack Honeybourne, girl is Betty Course next to girl in hat Joan Robbins. From right girl in hat Joan Pugh next to Dulcie Wells. Girl in centre back Cis Morgan. Mr William Richards is seated in the front.

Miss Crookes was a firm but fair teacher and was involved with many of the village activities. In the wintertime when there was a hard frost she would close the school and take the pupils skating on the pond by the vicarage or at Barrells Hall. She retired in 1924 and went to stay with her sister in Canada for a while. Miss Martha Seal and Mrs Mahoney followed on at the school, Mrs Mahoney rather fond of using the cane. She organised school concerts and once took the pupils on an outing to London by Midland Red Bus to see London Zoo and the Crown Jewels. Pupils had a

57

Christmas party with a Father Christmas and a Christmas tree and played musical chairs, pass the parcel and danced Roger de Coverley. Mrs Mary Friend who was Mary Squires at that time, came as a trainee teacher staying with her Uncle and Aunt, Mr and Mrs Charles Friend at Crowley's Farm. She went away to training college and taught for a while at Small Heath. She later married Dudley Friend and when there was a vacancy for Head Teacher she returned to the school and lived for a while at the school house before moving to Crowley's Farm.

Ullenhall School children.

A trainee teacher also at that time was Miss Emily Pace who continued at the school teaching the infants as a non certificated teacher. She married Mr Alfred Barret from Heath Farm and together Mrs Friend and Mrs Barret taught at Ullenhall School for well over thirty years.

In the 1940-50's the school day started with prayers and a hymn from the Golden Bells hymnbook. In the junior school room children were taught history, geography, english, maths (with 10 mental arithmetic questions) most mornings, art, nature study and reading. Boys would practise weaving on small looms while girls would do knitting and sewing with all pupils making raffia items.

After one of the lessons about Marco Polo and his travels and the discovery of silk, Mrs Friend managed to obtain some silkworms and kept them in a glass case so that pupils could observe the silk process. They were fed on mulberry leaves picked from the mulberry tree on the Vicarage lawn by Elizabeth Bird, grand daughter of Rev George Haywood.

On another occasion to illustrate a point Mrs Friend brought an orphan lamb from her farm, to school for the morning, taking it back again at dinnertime. In the summertime Mrs Barret would sometimes put one or two of the youngest infants out in the playground for a nap, on canvas fold up beds and cover them with a grey blanket.

From left, Mrs Barret with Mrs Crofts, Mrs Roden, Mrs Lilian Bell, Mrs Gladys Brockenshire..

Another lesson or activity in summertime was gardening. The school gardens were at the rear of the school house next to the school. Mrs Barret would take the girls and do the flower borders while Mrs Friend would take the boys to dig the vegetable gardens. Flowers such as candytuft, marigolds, nastursium and love in a mist were grown and seeds carefully saved for the next year. Much of the vegetable produce was sold at a reasonable price and the money put towards school funds.

At Christmas time there would be great excitement with the making of calendars and Christmas cards and yards of paper chains to decorate the schoolrooms. A Christmas party was held with a tree and a Father Christmas. Sandwiches, jellies and cakes were prepared by some parents and after these were eaten Mrs Friend would play the music for dancing Sir Roger de Coverley. Oranges and Lemons, Okey Cokey and other games.

During Mrs Friend's time at Ullenhall School it became impossible for the school managers to afford repairs and improvements needed, so in 1955 the school came under the County for the necessary work to be done, although retaining its church status. In 1960 a new extension was opened and a school playing field taken from Crowley's land. Mrs Friend played the church organ for thirty years and was a member of the Parochial Church Council for over forty and secretary for much of that time. She was a Parish Councillor and had a great knowledge of Ullenhall's history.

While the Rev Pelton was vicar of Ullenhall Mrs Pelton started a small private school at the vicarage, this school closed when Rev Pelton moved away.

Gordon Hemming as a young lad at Mrs Pelton's school, wearing his straw hat which he hated. The photograph was taken by Mr. Pelton.

Ullenhall School children 1948. *me!*
Front row from left - Michael Smalley, Carole Watton, John Cleaver, Rosemary Summers, Barbara Ross, Beverley Humphries, ?
Back row fron left - Jim Salmons, George Rogers, Marie Allcott, Kevin Humphries, Margaret Tomlin, Leslie Taylor, Sylvia Smith.

Ullenhall School and School House.

ULLENHALL CHURCH

St. Mary's parish church was built in Ullenhall by Mr T.H.G. Newton and his family in memory of their father and mother in 1875. The church cost £5,000 to build and was designed by Mr J. Seddon. The stone came from Chipping Campden, Gloucestershire and from Box, near Bath. The blue sand stone pillars came from a quarry near Bristol. Inside the church is a wooden barrel roof which has been compared to an up-turned boat. The curved sanctuary is unusual with a mosaic flooring incorporating the Christian symbol of the fish, as well as the cross and crown in the design. The lamp stands by the pew were the supports for the oil lamps which originally lit the church.

The church bells were cast by J. Warner & Son Ltd in London 1874. Numbers one to seven are inscribed "Come let us make a joyful noise", one word on each bell. The eighth bell the tenor, has the inscription "E.N." and "M.R.N." Elizabeth and Mary Rose Newton.

The first wedding in St. Mary's church in 1875 was of The Right Rev. Bishop of Sierra Leone to Mary Rose Newton. The couple must have embarked for Africa straightaway, arriving in Sierra Leone on February 1st in good health. However the marriage only lasted seven months for Mary Rose died on August 16th 1875 and was buried in Freetown, Sierra Leone.

View of St. Mary's Church Ullenhall.

Inside view of St. Mary's mistakenly called St. Mark's. This view shows the original oil lamps used for lighting the church.

In 1887 at Jubilee Mr Newton gave the village the Church Clock.

The Newton family fame to church driving along a carriage way from Barrells across the fields to a private entrance which was in the corner of the church where the organ now stands.

The music in the church was originally played on a harmonium. The present organ came from St. John's Church, Henley in 1914. The bellows were hand pumped, with some school boys having to take a turn of duty. Sometimes if they weren't attending to the service, the first few notes of the hymn were a bit squeaky until enough air was pumped in. The bellows of the organ were converted to electricity during the 1950's.

A good choir was established in the church and Ullenhall Choir won the Award of Merit for choir singing in 1929.

During Rev Haywards ministry several lay preachers came to the church to preach the sermon. One notable person being Sir Alfred Owen of the Rubery Owen organisation. He was a committed lay preacher and worked on many boards and committees such as Dr. Barnardo's and the Y.M.C.A. In 1949 B.R.M. was formed as a co-operative by Raymond Mays to build a great British racing car but after a series of disasters he sold out to Sir Alfred Owen. The B.R.M. car was going to be Britain's answer to Maserati Porshe etc., and there were high hopes and expectations for its success. Sir Alfred Owen took the letters B.R.M. in a biblical sense as the basis for his sermon, thus ensuring that the project was kept in people's minds.

The Shield won by Ullenhall Church Choir in 1929.

ULLENHALL VICARAGE

The vicarage was built by the Newton family in 1875 and cost £2,000. The architect Mr J. Seddon designed it in the Gothic style. There was an octagonal central hall with a black and white tiled floor. Leading off this was a study, drawing room, dining room, kitchen, scullery and staff room. On the first floor were five bedrooms leading from an octagonal galleried landing and on the second floor were two attics. It was situated in approximately an acre of ground and within short walking distance across the field to the church.

The Vicars of Ullenhall.

Richard Thursfield 1862 - 72
John George 1873 - 78
Melbourne Russel West 1879 - 99
Loton Parry 1899 - 1901
William Frederick Pelton 1901 - 32
Frank Ridley Whittaker 1932 - 42
William Godfrey Cooper 1943 - 1944
George Hayward 1945 - 55
Thomas H. Evans 1955 -

Ullenhall Vicarage.

January 1900

A presentation to Rev. West took place at his home in Leamington. A clock, garniture, Century Dictionary, silver candlesticks and sewing machine were presented by churchwardens Mr T. Newton and Mr T.A. Wilkes.

Monday 15 Jan 1900.

Rev. Loton Parry is appointed. A celebration tea took place in the school room, 130 people sat down. Mr Newton asked people to pray for the four men who had gone to the front in South Africa, one of the four being Mr Newton's son. Mr Newton gave a hearty welcome to their new Vicar and urged people to rally round him.

Of all the vicars of Ullenhall Mr Pelton was the longest serving and perhaps the most controversial. His outdoor wear was a long cloak and he is still remembered for his habit of walking up and down the vicarage lawn composing his sermon, with his long cloak flapping in the breeze. He was said not to take kindly to children making a noise in church or if anyone had a tickly cough.

Stratford Herald. April 1905.

Sir, - In connection with the Ullenhall controversy my daughter's name has been used, and your readers have no doubt wondered why such spleen should be shown from the vicar of a parish towards his teachers.

Now, Sir, it is not my purpose to venture on an explanation, but simply to state a few facts relative to my position as organist. For some reason he has been for some time past very anxious to remove my daughter from the organ, as evidenced by the many petty annoyances and almost insults to which she has been submitted. For instance, some of the members of the choir misbehaved, and the organist, together with the rest, received a long letter of reproof written in a very dictatorial style! She has also had much trouble regarding hymn lists etc., and recently he has denied her the use of the organ for practice unless his special permission were obtained. Then came the threat of a prosecution for conveying influenza to Ullenhall, which has been proved to have no foundation in fact, for the village was already infected - a fact which should soon be discovered by the clergy of a parish. After trying in vain to force her resignation and even asking (or rather dictating) my help in the matter, he apparently called upon the Rural Dean to accomplish the feat through the church wardens.

If Miss Crookes has suffered similar annoyance and persecution, one cannot be surprised that a bitter feeling has been engendered.

My advice to my daughter is to leave the village and seek a place where a more Christian feeling dominates the shepherd of the flock.
I am Sir, faithfully yours, F. Furnival.

Ullenhall Vicarage,
June 1929.

My dear Friends,

Two events have happened recently, which are in themselves occasions of great joy. One is that the members of the Women's Working Party have most generously made a gift of £10 towards the purchase of a new boiler required for the church - - a gift that contrasts most favourably with the general absence of response to my appeal made some years ago when £60 was required for a new warming apparatus. The other event is the confirmation at St. Martin's when eight candidates were presented from this parish, making eighteen altogether in two years. So far nothing could be more Gratifying.

But there is unfortunately another side to each event of quite a different character. We have had a spell of glorious weather in consequence of which the attendance at Church had suffered greatly, and the collections have fallen 40%. As regards the money, it will not require many Sunday of the same kind to wipe off completely the gift mentioned above, and leave the Church as poor as ever. While as regards the attendance, the consequence are in my estimation still more serious.

The only question that I ever feel justified in asking candidates for confirmation, who attend my classes regularly and appear to be attentive is, do you desire an additional means of grace? Do you value those you already enjoy so highly as to desire another? Yet what has happened immediately after the service. On the very first Sunday most of them went for a walk instead of attending church as I am sorry to say last year's candidates generally do. Moreover, with some two or three exceptions it is quite unusual to see any of the latter at a celebration. The fault of course, lies originally with their seniors, parents, and neighbours, many of whom set them a wholly bad example. If all the regular communicants, who are few in number, happen to be absent, then no celebration can be held - - as was the case on Ascension Day and Trinity Sunday, not to mention other occasions only last winter.

My object in calling your attention to such matters - - not for the first time - is that I have accepted them as the will of God that I should leave this parish, as I shall do shortly in order to make room for someone else who, I hope, will meet with more success than I have done. No parish can possibly thrive when the attendance at Church falls down to a few dozen, and the collections for the day amount to about sixteen shillings, as was the case last Sunday. I also hope that no one will think it worth while to make any parting gift, as is often made to a retiring Vicar, for if my words had had the desired effect I should not be contemplating moving on. I have always been strongly opposed to any *occasional* effort when it is merely a substitute for continuous support which the Church urgently needs. A few have been doing their best, and most valuable their help has been; but they are too few for the Church to thrive.

Before I came here everything had been kept in the hands of one family,who were willing under such conditions to keep the Church out of debt. Consequently other parishioners failed to realize that the Church belonged to them as well, or took any pride in it; and with such an example before their eyes, new arrivals in the Parish have naturally been prone to treat it with the same indifference. All would be more or less sorry no doubt for the doors to be closed, but the majority shirk all responsibility in the matter.

Possibly your next Vicar may by God's grace be more successful in teaching you that the parish Church belongs to the Parishioners and should be supported by them.

Sincerely yours,
W.F. Pelton

EXTRACT FROM KELLY'S DIRECTORY - 1892

ULLENHALL, in Domesday "Holehale," and later, "Oulenhall," and Aspley, hamlets of the parish of Wootton Wawen, were constituted a separate ecclesiastical parish, June 27, 1861, and are on the Worcestershire border, 2 miles north-west from Henley-in-Arden, 10 north-west from Stratford-on-Avon, and 6 north-west from Bearley station on the Birmingham and Stratford section of the Great Western railway, in the South-Western division of the county, Barlichway hundred, Henley petty sessional division, Stratford-on-Avon union and county court district, Alcester rural deanery and archdeaconry and diocese of Worcester. The chapel of St. Mary, dating from the 14th century, served until lately as the parish church, but is now used only as a mortuary chapel; it consists simply of a chancel and nave, and has few attractive features, save, perhaps a singular Decorated window in the south wall of three trefoiled lights, but destitute of any hood-moulding: there remains some fragments of ancient glass and encaustic tiles, and in the chancel are mural monuments to Francis Throckmorton, of Coughton Court esq. circ. 1553-8, and to Robert Knight, Earl of Catherlough in the peerage of Ireland, d. 30 March, 1772: there are also monuments to this family in the church of Wootton Wawen, but the bodies of the persons mentioned, at first interred there, and subsequently in a mausoleum in Barrells Park, were eventually buried at Ullenhall: the modern parish church, situated near the village, is an edifice of Bath and Campden stone, in the Decorated style, erected in 1875 by the Newton family, from designs by J. P. Seddon esq. of London, and consists of apsidal chancel, nave, aisles, transepts, north porch and a western tower with spire, containing 8 bells: there are 250 sittings, 100 being free. The register dates from the year 1840. The living is a vicarage, average tithe rent-charge £92; net yearly value £60, with residence, erected in 1875, in the gift of T. H. G. Newton esq. and held since 1879 by the Rev. Melbourne Russell West M.A. of Queen's College, Oxford. The Charities amount to about £75 a year. Barrells Hall, formerly the residence of the Earls of Catherlough, and now the seat of Thomas Henry Goodwin Newton esq. J.P. is in a well-wooded park of 400 acres. T. H. G. Newton esq. who is lord of the manor, George Frederick Muntz esq. D.L., J.P. of Umberslade, Hockley Heath, and the trustees of the late late Rev. Henry Charles Knight M.A. of Malvern Wells, are the principal landowners. The soil is mixed, consisting of clay, gravel and marl; subsoil, various. The chief crops are wheat, barley and pasturage. The area is 2,933a. 3r. 18p.; the population in 1891 was 503.

Parish Clerk, Thomas Franklin.

Post Office.—Miss Catharine Cooke, receiver. Letters arrive from Birmingham via Henley-in-Arden at 8.10 a.m.; dispatched at 5.35 p.m. The nearest money order & telegraph office is at Henley-in-Arden. Postal orders are issued here but not paid

National School (mixed), built in 1876 for 86 children; average attendance, 68; Miss Ellen Hodgkin, mistress

Carriers.—George Tomlin, to Birmingham, mon. thurs. & sat. to Stratford-on-Avon, friday; & Fred Tomlin from Bird-in-Hand, Beaudesert, to Birmingham, thursday

Cockle Mrs. The Brook house
Newton Thomas Henry Goodwin M.A. J.P. Barrells Hall
Newton Miss, Heath lodge
West Rev. Melbourne Russell M.A. Vicarage
Bagshawe Fredk. Geo. farmer, Impsley
Barnstable Fras. farmer, Merriman's lil
Burman Thomas, farmer, Nutlands
Caldicott Arthur Cotterell, agent to T. H. G. Newton esq
Cattell Thos. Randell. farmer, Ford hall
Cooke Catherine (Miss), shopkeeper, Post office
Deakin Wm. Hy. farmer, Halland
Docker George, farmer, Trap's green
Docker James, jun. farmer, Trap's green
Dutton Henry, cowkeeper
Edwards Isaac, boot maker & farmer, Trap's green
Franklin Charles, farmer
Harris Joseph Hy. farmer (Fosters)
Hemming Thomas, blacksmith
Hill William, farm bailiff to the trustees of the late Rev. Hy. C. Knight M.A., J.P
Hind John, shopkeeper & baker
Lee Arthur, farmer
Ma;yon John, farmer, College farm
Podmore George, cooper & wheelwright
Pugh Joseph Davies, boot & shoe makr
Reader Mark, farmer, Blunt's green
Reader William, farmer, Trap's green
Rushton Marianne (Mrs.), farmer, Rose cottage
Taylor Richard, farmer, James' farm
Taylor Thomas, farmer, Botley hill
Taylor William, farmer
Tomlin George, carrier
Tomlin John, farmer, Blunt's green
Tomlin William, farmer, Chapel gates
Turner Edwin, farmer, Aspley
Ullenhall CoffeeHouse(Wm.Tyler,man)
Walker Walter, Wings & Spur inn
White Charles, farmer
Winter Alfred, machinist
Wilks Thos. Arthur, farmer, Meat ho
Working Men's Club & Library (Richard Smith, sec)

THE VILLAGE

The parish of Ullenhall in the 1920-30's comprised mainly farmland with the farms situated around the village. People did a lot of walking or went by pony trap or bicycle if they were lucky enough to have one. The railway station at Danzey was about two miles away and men who caught the train to work and those who worked on the railway itself usually walked through Mockley Wood. After the railway had been built in 1906 people would come out from Birmingham to Danzey Station for a day out in the popular Mockley Woods. It was a very pleasant wood in those days with large oak trees, hazel nut bushes, ferns and a carpet of bluebells in the season. They would bring a picnic lunch and stay for the day.

Ullenhall Village.

Ullenhall Village showing the cottage behind the Winged Spur which was later demolished to make a car park. Also demolished were the three soil toilets, one gents, one ladies and one junior.

Post Office and Blacksmiths shop, Ullenhall.

Ullenhall Village before the Central Stores were built.

Bottom of village with the Coffee House on the left.

Shop at top of the village.

Bluebells in Mockley Woods.

A day out in Mockley Woods.

Perry Mill cottages, Ullenhall. Late 1890-1900. The white posts show position of a culvert.

Keeping Water Lane tidy before it was tarmaced.

Perry Mill 1930's.

Water Lane from village end with the wooden footbridge to avoid the mud.

Delivering milk at the Perry Mill

Milking time Watery Lane, 1930's. The lane has now been tarmaced. The girl is Cis Morgan, the boy Derek Richmond.

Ralph Franklin and Cis Morgan pumping water.

Many wives in those days kept and dressed chickens and some made butter which was often taken to the Wednesday market at Henley. People had large gardens and some had allotments to grow their own vegetables. In the days before the railway farm produce was taken into Birmingham every week by carrier cart.

Cattle were walked to the market at Henley when they had to be sold, smaller animals were taken by horse drawn float. Many people also kept their own pig and a Mr Tom Hughes walked from Tanworth to kill the pigs, not always turning up on the appointed day. In later years Bill Harris and Beck Harris from Henley came round and introduced the humane killer which was a blessing after the throat cutting of the pigs.

FARMER'S GLORY

The hours of gold come back to me
That Time has pinched (he can't return 'em),
The well-remembered chestnut tree
(Or was it, after all, laburnum?)
The rural rill,
The shriek of dying pigs — I hear them still.

Once a year the policeman from Tanworth would cycle down to Ullenhall to check on dog and gun licences.

Hay was cut by horsedrawn mower then turned by hand, pitched onto the cart then unloaded to the rick builder who would later thatch it.

The roadsides were kept tidy by the roadmen, they were given lengths and scythed the grass verges and edged them with a spade also keeping the ditches and drains cleaned out. When the roads were tarmaced, the hot tar was poured on the road then large chippings thrown over, followed by the steam roller. In the very hot weather the tar would ooze through the chippings creating havoc with people's footwear.

In the very hot summers water would be in short supply, for those who still had their own pump water it wasn't such a problem, but for the people who were on mains water the supply was a bit hit or miss. The water came from a borehole at the top of the village by Crowley's Farm but the people on mains water supply at the other end of the village would sometimes find a muddy trickle coming out of the taps. Every drop of water would be saved, tea leaves, washing up water and water from the soft water butts in order to keep the vegetables growing.

One of the special events in Ullenhall during the 1920's was a vist of the mop who were called Rocky Herberts in the small field on the corner of Church Hill. There were roundabouts, swings, shooting and coconut shies, also homemade boiled sweets. It was a family concern with father, mother, daughter and husband with two mall boys.

Some time later on the walk through the village by Fosset's Circus always created a buzz of excitement. The circus would make overnight quarters along the route to their next engagement and would sometimes use the stable block at Barrells Hall to rest the animals. There was great hilarity among the children when Alice, the elephant, walking through the village, put her trunk in the back of the bakers van and took a loaf of bread.

During the 1939-45 war German planes could be heard overhead on their way to bomb Birmingham and other towns. On 14th November 1940 the Germans bombed Coventry which was the centre of British war production. It was said that the glow in the night sky from the resultant fire could be seen from miles around. One Ullenhall resident upon hearing the planes going over and the bombs being dropped automatically ducked for the nearest cover which happened to be a row of old runner beans!

Whilst many farms had working horses to do the farmwork with, gradually using tractors etc., one farmer, Mr Wilkinson from Yew Tree Farm kept a horse for showing. He had always been interested in horses and had a half bred hackney x Welsh Cob called 'Ullenhall Flare'. He won many prizes but his main delight was when he won at the Three Counties Show. He also won prizes at Coventry, Fillongley and Handsworth. He used to show either as a 'Private Turnout' with the gig or a 'Tradesmans Turnout' with the float.

Ploughing time.

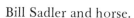

Bill Sadler and horse.

John Wilkinson, Yew Tree Farm, Ullenhall with "Ullenhall Flare".

The appearance of the village changed relatively slowly during the first half of this century. Four council houses were built on Church Hill in the 1920's, followed by twelve council houses on the other side of the road in the 1930's. These had three bedrooms, a cold water supply with the bath in the kitchen and an outside toilet. The curious thing about the houses was that they were built back to front. The front door overlooked the fields and the approach to them from Church Hill was up the garden path to the back door. It was said that the landowner who sold the ground didn't want the view of washing hanging out.

The other major development in the village was the building of twelve houses in St. Mark's Close in 1949. The architect Mr Francis Yorke who lived at Park Barn at that time, later won a Design Award for the project. Some houses were built in the 1950's along the Henley Road linking what was then the end bungalow in Ullenhall to the Lodge at the entrance gates of Barrells Hall.

9

Church Hill, Ullenhall with some of the council houses.

VILLAGE ACTIVITIES

Sunday was usually spent by going to church, with the children going to Sunday School as well in the afternoon. The Sunday School children were sometimes taken on outings to local places such as Yarningale Common, having games on the common and tea at a nearby tea toom, also visiting the Lickey Hills. Older girls belonged to the G.F.S. (Girls Friendly Society) which was a branch of the Henley society. The girls did sewing and crochet work, seagrass weaving on stool seats and some country dancing. They also had outings such as a visit to Claverdon in Ralph Franklin's pony and trap. They were also taken to see Coventry Cathedral. (This was the original Cathedral before it was bombed in the second World War.

1935 was the Silver Jubilee year of King George V and Queen Mary, and a horse drawn wagon with the Queen and attendants started from Crowley's Farm down the village to a field at Brook House where such sports as races, barrel boxing and pillow fighting sitting on a pole was followed by tea in a marquee. Children were presented with commemoration mugs by Mrs Barrett from Heath Farm. The celebrations finished with a bonfire being lit on the allotment field. During the day there was

81

also country dancing, the girls wearing dresses made from material provided by Mr Friend of Crowley's Farm. The sun shone and all together it was a very happy day.

Ralph Franklin with pony and trap and passengers.

Silver Jubilee celebrations 1935. Ken Portman as Mr. Brown and Mrs Ross as Queen Victoria.

Coronation celebrations.

The 1937 Coronation was more spectacular, organised by Mrs Peace from Rose Cottage.   There were four horse drawn wagons, the first was Brittania with attendants, the other wagons held people of the Empire and Eastern countries.   Refreshments were served in the new Village Hall which was opened in 1935, but unfortunately the weather was not very good.

The Women's Institute started in 1927, meeting at first in the schoolroom before transferring to the new Village Hall.

At the official opening of the Village Hall in 1935 Mr Siddall-Jones announced that Mrs Pelton the widow of a former Vicar had given £100 and also Mrs Matthews, a former resident at Grimshaw had also given £100.   Mr & Mrs W.L. Barber who lived at that time in Grimshaw gave the gift of the land and a donation of £500.   The total cost of the Hall was £1,500, the rest of the money being raised by the Whist Drives and dances which had been held at the Coffee House.

When motorised vehicles became more available day trips by coach were organised by Mrs Hetty Tomlin to seaside towns such as Aberystwyth, Rhyl, Weston-super-Mare and to Blackpool Illuminations, staying at the same hotel for twenty years.

Women's Institute.

The opening of the Village Hall.

Trip to Blackpool. Front row, left to right, Mrs Archer, Mrs Hetty Tomlin, Mrs Watkins, also present are Mr. & Mrs Wilkinson, Hazel and Norma Wilkinson, Mr. Watkins, Joe Tomlin, Fred Tomlin, Mr. & Mrs Bill Harris.

The Home Guard was formed in 1941, previously being called Local Defence Volunteers. At first they were without guns but practised parade drill on the ground behind the Village Hall, before the first Tennis Court was built. They had to use whatever was available in order to practise sloping arms etc., these included brooms, hoes and muck forks. Unfortunately, one of the men using a muck fork was not sure of his left from right so that whoever was next to him in the line up had to be prepared to duck swiftly. Eventually they were issued with the real thing.

A great delight in winter was sledging on Stankley. At one time corn was grown on the field, with the horse drawn binder going round the field until a small piece was left in the middle of the field. Men from the village would stand round the edges of the field waiting for rabbits to run out from this last refuge. The sheaves of corn were put in stooks around the field waiting for the threshing machine. When the snow came children would sledge down the slope in the field sometimes at night time by lamplight, occasionally parents would come too.

Home Guard. This photograph was taken at Henley with some Henley Home Guard men. Centre front row, Fred Tomlin, Mr. Lakin. 2nd row, right to left, Austen Taylor, James Millward, Jim Lamb. Third row centre, Les Richmond. Back row, right to left, Peter Lawson, Gordon Hemming, Les Hancox.

Tawny Owl, Winnifred Archer's wedding to
Stanley Richmond from Dean's Green.
Brownies, top left, Brenda Jackson, Rosemary
Summers, Sylvia Smith. Top right, Barbara
Ross, Elizabeth Bird, Diana Lewis.

A Brownie group was started in the village in 1929 and continued
for a number of years. When Rev. Haywood came to the village, his
daughter Mrs Kathleen Bird re-started the Brownie group with meetings
held in the school room. Mrs Bird became Brown Owl and Winnifred
Archer Tawny Owl. On Tawny Owl's wedding day the Brownies formed
a guard of honour outside the church.

Mrs Franklin's dances.

Mrs Franklin originally came to Ullenhall to stay with her nephew
who worked at Mount Pleasant Farm. She became involved with the
dances at the Village Institute, then at the Village Hall, eventually coming
to live in the caretakers cottage at the Institute which was later called
Arden Cottage. She was an ex-Tiller Girl and held weekly ballet and tap
dancing lessons for children at the Village Hall. At one dancing display
during the 1940's performed at a Church Fete at Mrs Fudge's home
'Greenacres' with the dress material being on ration, the children's
dresses were made from crepe paper and some of the ladies frilly dresses
were made from black out material.

87

Dancing display at 'Greenacres'. From left Alice Allcott, Gladys Taylor, Joyce Morrell, Beryl Sly, Nancy Tomlin, Celia Lewis, Norma Wilkinson, Hazel Wilkinson.

Mrs Franklin's dancers. Mrs Franklin's partner is Don Howell. Sitting on stage left to right is Ray Davis, Celia Adshead, Sue Salmons, Hazel Goodman, Christine Cox, Brian McKenna, David Chapman, Rosemary Summers, Sheila Chalmers. Second row, left to right is ?, Maureen Holt, Sheila Tomlin, David Cox, Jean Clayton, Sandra Lewis, Keith Merryfield, Julia Pepper, Basil Tisor, John Summers. Back row, left to right, ?, ?, Doris Amey, ?, Charles Amey, ?.

Mrs Franklin also held dances at the Village Hall on a Saturday night. Mr Bill Harris secretary of the Village Hall would prepare the floor by shaving bits off a white candle on to the area where the dancers circled round. The music came from 78 r.p.m. records, played on a black wind up gramophone. There were many Victor Sylvestor records playing dance music for the slow foxtrot, waltz, quickstep, palais glide, lancers, Paul Jones etc. Sometimes when a dance was in full swing the gramophone would wind down and someone had to quickly jump on to the stage and wind it up. The dances were very popular with people coming from many outlying parts of the village making it an ideal way for them to meet. People walked or came by bicycle even one couple coming by car from Hall Green. Looking back it seems incredible that so much enjoyment was found with such simple means.

The dances continued until the early 1950's but as people started to stay in more to watch television and cars became available people were able to find other pleasures. Mrs Franklin continued to hold dances on a Tuesday night which were partly instructive.

The Tennis Club 1930's. Back row, left to right, Madge Lenton, Les Wells, Mary Pugh, Nancy Tomlin, Stan Pugh, Flor Morgan. Front row, left to right, Cis Morgan, Dulcie Wells, Joan Pugh, ?.

The Tennis Club.

In the 1930's the tennis enthusiasts in the village did not have their own particular piece of ground to play on. At one time some ground next to Miss Steeley's cottage was used. The tennis players would cut the grass and roll the ground flat themselves and after school this piece of ground was popular with the boys, to gather and have a punch up.

The Tennis Club then used a field belonging to Mr Siddall-Jones at Brook House for a while, after this they made a tennis lawn in 'Nip' Allcott's field by the side of Watery Lane.

The Tennis Club as it is today was started by Mrs Celia Lewis in 1949 with a loan from the Village Hall. A hard court was built behind the Village Hall, since then a second hard court has been built and the Tennis Club has gone from strength to strength.

Amateur Dramatics

Mr Rowland Jones from the Central Stores was very interested in amateur drama and helped with many productions at the Village Hall. He started the Ullenhall Players who are still going strong. He was also a parish council member for 25 years, of which he was chairman for 12 years, also being chairman of the school governors for 25 years.

Coronation 1953

The 1953 Coronation of Queen Elizabeth II was celebrated in the village between watching television. There was a wagon with Queen and attendants, pulled by a tractor, followed by decorated bicycles and fancy dress. A display of country dancing was held in the centre of the village and tea was provided in the Village Hall. The weather was quite chilly and not many people went to watch the sports in a downpour of rain. All the children were given Coronation mugs.

THE ULLENHALL PUBLIC HOUSE

The first record of a public house in Ullenhall is the Catherlough Arms in 1772, which replaced a small house previously called the Catherlough Arms. The original Catherlough Arms was situated in Henley-in-Arden in 1771 with eight acres of land and jointly occupied by Thomas Tibbatts, Edward Graves and Abraham Winspur. In 1781 there was a public house called 'The Talbot' in Ullenhall, perhaps making two in the village. In 1808 John Greaves kept the Catherlough Arms and in 1813 his widow Mary Greaves was the landlady. It was still called the

Catherlough Arms in 1818 but by 1856 for some reason it became the Spur Inn, kept by Robert Tatham and in 1859 James Salt became the landlord.

In 1874 the public house was known as the Spur and Wing Inn, with landlord William Turner and on January 15th 1887 the license of the Spur Inn was transferred from William Turner to Felicia Turner.

In 1894 it was known as the Wings and Spur Inn with landlord Walter Walker. He was the butler at Barrells Hall until he retired to take on the pub. He died in 1918 and was succeeded by his son William Walker, who had previously been head gardener at Barrells Hall. In 1932 Sidney Payne was landlord at the pub by then being called the Winged Spur. Lawrence Hunt known as 'Lol' Hunt followed on until the 1960's with Jack Hoad succeding him.

Friday July 30th 1886

On Sunday evening last an old man named Thomas Taylor who had lived at Ullenhall nearly all his life, hung himself from a hook in the ceiling of his house. He had placed a stool under the hook for this purpose. Deceased was quite well as usual on Sunday last, having attended Church both morning and evening and no cause can be assigned for destroying himself.

An inquest was held on his body at the Spur Inn.

THE VILLAGE SHOPS

In the latter part of the 19th century and the early part of the 20th century Ullenhall had a variety of shops in the village and also a variety of trades were carried on. There was a bakery and grocers shop, a boot and shoe maker, a cooper and wheelright, a blacksmiths, a Post Office and general stores and a public house, the Winged Spur. Also in the late 19th century and until after the 1914/18 War Mr Fritz Heaphy and Mr John Morris cycled from Redditch each month around the village to collect orders for their tailors and grocery shops with a van delivering the goods in a few days time.

At the turn of the century Mr Tatnall kept a grocery and drapers shop at the top of the village with a bakehouse attached, kept by Mr and Mrs Chataway. Mr John Allcott worked at this bakery before establishing his own bakery and grocery shop at the bottom of the village. He won many cups and awards for his bread and pork pies. He also kept pigs at the rear of the bakery to eat any leftovers. After he retired his grandson John Merryfield lived there and started a boat building business on the bakery premises.

Mr. & Mrs Tatnall outside the shop about 1918. Girls are, left to right, Ivy Gordon, Dorothy Wells, Grace Neal, Rita Gould.

Mr. Allcott's bakery shop.

The 'Arden Table Water' business was started by Mr Sidney Taylor behind Mr Allcott's shop but later moved to Henley. The bakery at the top of the village closed but the grocery part of the business was sold (1932) to Mr Stephen Impey. He later started the first taxi business in Ullenhall with a canvas topped Austin Seven.

Pop!

That GOOD Healthy sound that tells you there is life in the bottle.

Arden Mineral Waters

The Purest and most Carefully Bottled.

Manufactured only at

HENLEY-IN-ARDEN.

The wedding of Evelyn Grace Richards, post-mistress, to William Laughton Sparrow. He died in 1946 leaving her a widow for 35 years.

The Post Office in Ullenhall was kept by a Miss Catherine Cooke in 1892, followed by Mr Washington Richards until 1936 then carried on by his daughter Mrs Evelyn Sparrow. The first public telephone in Ullenhall was in the Post Office, then later moved to a kiosk outside. Telegrams were frequently sent as there were few other telephones in the village. Most things that people were likely to want were sold in the shop, shoe and household polishes, washing powder, soaps, snuff, twist, mousetraps, cottons and tapes, leather shoelaces, hair nets, groceries, biscuits loose in tins, cakes that had often got a notice on 'Fresh in' or 'Cheap to clear'. There was a big hand worked bacon machine on the counter by the window. On the right hand side in the shop was the post office. The letters were sorted on the kitchen table ready for the postman. Mr Tommy Stanton was the postman for a number of years walking miles to collect and deliver the post. Later on Mr Dipple delivered the post by bicycle. He always sat on a chair on the left just inside and was given a cup of tea when he collected the afternoon mail. There were also jars of sweets which would be weighed out in paper cones, boxes of chocolates and on the right of the shop were bags with dog biscuits and chicken feed, a convenience for people who kept a few chickens. Torch batteries, pencils, ink and writing paper, birthday cards to name some of the items sold leaving only a small gangway for customers. In the window display was a selection of non-perishable goods crayoning books, jigsaw puzzles etc. On a sunny day a cat would lie in the window display sunning itself. A cyclist would collect papers from Danzey Station and these were sorted on the kitchen table before being sold.

Post Office and War Memorial.

F.J.S. Clayton, only son of the blacksmith W. Clayton, youngest of 8 girls. He took up shoe repairing, using the front room of Mr. & Mrs Joe Tomlin's cottage, now Old Turf Cottage. Octavia Clayton was married at St. Mary's to Thomas Latham of Studley who worked for Mr. Allcott, the baker.

Next to the Post Office was the blacksmiths shop, a place of interest to young and old.   The blacksmith was Mr Clayton while his wife kept a shoe and secondhand clothes shop in the cottage at the rear of the Winged Spur.   (This was later demolished to make way for the car park). At the cottage opposite to the Winged Spur, a Mr Hubble had a small dairy.   Mr Loach from Redditch bought the cottage afterwards and opened a fish and chip shop (1924).   When the cottage again changed hands Mr Morgan started a garage business there.   It was called Sunnyside Electrics and had two petrol pumps.   He was a signalman on the railway and also repaired bicycles and tyres and charged wireless accumulator batteries.   He sold the business in 1950 to Jim and Celia Lewis who demolished the cottage to make way for a new garage building and forecourt.

View of Ullenhall showing cottage next to the school, once the fish and chip shop.

Mr Leonard Course had a haberdashery and greengrocery shop at Church View in the 1930's and later built the Central Stores in what was the garden to Church View.   The Central Stores was bought by Mr Rowland Jones in 1936 who developed the grocery and greengrocery business and bought a van to develop a delivery round.   Mr and Mrs Homer moved to Church View and kept a small haberdashery business for a time but this eventually closed although Mr and Mrs Homer continued to live there.

Mr. Hill's workshop with caravan at rear. Man in front with hat is William Washington Richards, girl is Gladys Taylor, boy is Eric Reader.

After the blacksmiths shop had closed down Mr Sid Hill used the building for storage for his handyman business. He lived in a caravan with his wife and daughter, at the rear of the blacksmiths shop but there was some controversy about the siting of the caravan.

When the blacksmiths shop became vacant again it was then used by Ullenhall Egg Supplies. This business was started by Fred Tomlin and involved collecting eggs for three days around the Cotswolds and three days distributing them to outlets in Birmingham. The eggs were candled first in a darkened room, by rolling them through a box with small holes in, under which was a powerful bulb which shone through the eggs and showed any imperfections.

The blacksmiths shop was sold to Mr Billy Peace a local builder so the sorting and candling of the eggs was done in the front room of Fred Tomlin's mother's cottage opposite. However one day while taking his fiancee Nesta George home to Birmingham on his motorbike they had an accident. He suffered a broken leg and ribs and was taken to Birmingham Accident Hospital, Nesta George was knocked unconscious and taken to Dudley Road Hospital. Fred Tomlin's future brother-in-law Ken Portman was pressed into service to drive the van for the egg business. He had never driven a van before, only having had a motorbike. Luckily there was not much traffic on the roads in those days and all went well, especially when he had discovered what to do with the handbrake. The van was a Morris Commercial Van with two large headlamps on top of the front windows. One day while driving in Birmingham coming out of Bell Street and through the Bullring with the stalls on either side, one of the headlamps caught in a stall selling wreaths and carried them away. The stallholder ran after the van yelling "Bring my wreaths back", or words to that effect!

A Doctor's Surgery was held by Dr. Farr from Henley in a room at the cottage at the rear of The Winged Spur, then occupied by Mrs James. She would fill an enamel bucket with water for Dr. Farr to fill his medicine bottles. When the cottage was demolished the surgery moved to Mrs Tatnall's cottage. Mrs Tatnall had sold the shop to Mr Impey but she had the coach house and loft converted to living accommodation. The patients to see the doctor would sit and wait in her living room.

ULLENHALL IN WARTIME

Visit by the wife of the United States President, Mrs Roosevelt, to the land army girls at Oldberrow.

REGAL

Mrs. Roosevelt looked almost too regal for the cowshed; but all the animals wore black, and all had names. The front row consisted of Buttercup, Prunella, Helen, Fussy, Colleen, Hazel, Carnation and Patricia. Barbara Bishop, of Henley, and Helen Purver, of Kineton, were busy milking and demonstrated both hand and machine methods.

Once again Mrs. Roosevelt mounted the tractor-drawn lorry and proceeded down the road and across a bumpy field to see the mangold-pullers, the hedgers and ditchers and ploughing by Caterpillar tractors.

At the conclusion of the demonstration Mrs Roosevelt returned to the Hostel. She thanked the driver of the tractor and told her she was a "grand driver". Incidentally, Lady Reading, head of the W.V.S., accompanied Mrs. Roosevelt all the time.

Mrs. Roosevelt was conducted round the farm by Mr. E.J. Ballinger, farm manager to Mr. E.H. Smith of Grimshaw Hill.

INTRODUCTIONS

Before leaving, Mrs. Roosevelt was introduced to various heads of departments, including Miss Rotherham, vice-chairman of the Warwickshire Women's Land Army; Miss Diana Hunter, secretary of the Warwickshire Women's Land Army; Mr. Clyde Higgs, chairman of the Mechanical and Farm Management sub-committee of the War Agricultural Executive Committee; Mr. A.F. Haynes, chairman of the Labour sub-committee of the War Agricultural Executive Committee; and Mr. Arthur Tickle, chairman of the Warwickshire branch of the National Farmer's Union.

Miss Irene Birch, an art student before the War, who had volunteered for the Women's Land Army in 1939, presented Mrs. Roosevelt with a memento of her visit in the form of a red deerskin album of Land Army photographs, bearing the Women's Land Army badge on the cover.

The seven cars, headed by Mrs. Roosevelt's huge Chrysler, with the flag of the Stars and Stripes, proceeded down the road for another engagement before lunch - where, nobody knew. The Land Girls cheered and then went back to work. Everybody voted it a perfect morning. The sun seemed pleased too.

* * *

Farmer Roosevelt's wife - the President recently described himself as a farmer - rode about in a - - - cart yesterday to see Britain's Land Army girls.

She watched 200 of them parade, saw them milk, plough, thatch and ditch in Shakespeare's country, Warwickshire.

In the black coat, hat and shoes that she has constantly worn on her tour, and sitting on a rug over straw, she jogged over the fields in the tractor driven cart.

As it bumped and pitched on rough ground, small boys ran around.

Driver of the tractor was 23-year-old Margaret Browett, former Leicestershire office worker.

Mrs. Roosevelt visited a Land Army hostel for 35 girls, who are hired out to local farmers in the Oldberrow district near Henley-in-Arden.

She called at a twelfth century farm, and farm bailiff Balinger sat on the haycart beside her and answered her technical questions.

At the farm she saw cows being milked and a demonstration of thatch-making by machine by four land girls.

PLOUGHING GIRLS

Some of the farm equipment came from America and is similar to that used on the Roosevelt land.

Afterwards Mrs. Roosevelt went across the fields to see girls ploughing and cutting kale for cattle.

Thirteen-year-old Barry Yearsley, who belongs to a boy farmers' club, clambered aboard the haycart with an autograph book. Mrs. Roosevelt said "Certainly - so long as there aren't too many of you" and signed the book shakily as the cart moved on.

Lady Denham, Land Army chief, told her what the girls earn and how they are trained. "How interested my husband will be when I tell him about all this" - Mrs. Roosevelt said.

Later yesterday she toured a fighter factory employing large numbers of women - 40 per cent of their total workers. The girls did not stop work but clanged a welcome with their tools on their lathes and benches.

Land girls helping with the harvest. From left to right, Gordon Hemming, Austen Taylor and Bill Sadler.

Harvest time.

THE PAGEANT OF ULLENHALL

In 1959 A Pageant of Ullenhall was produced by Rev. T. Evans and held in the field at Grimshaw. The opening speech was given by The Lord Bishop of Coventry who was joined by an overseas visitor The Agent General of Queensland Mr D.J. Muir. The majority of village people played a part, their characters ranging from Celtic people of Ullenhall to residents of Barrells Hall and Crowleys. The event was supported by the Coventry Cathedral Choir with a parade of Veteran cars, the North Warwickshire Hunt and a parade of London Fashion Models. There was also Maypole dancing by Ullenhall school children and folk dancers from Hampton-in-Arden.

Village people in the Pageant. Left to right, Rosemary Tisor, Basil Tisor, Mrs Friend, Martin Friend, Mrs Lilian Bell, Flo Morgan, Mrs Duckworth, Sheila Cox.

Peter Wild, Mrs Doris Amey, Mrs Hetty Tomlin.

Mounted riders in the Pageant, Diana Lewis on
Smokey, Sandra Lewis on Merlin and Sheila
Tomlin on Rajah.

Mavis Tomlin and Jean Clayton in one of the
Vintage cars at the Pageant.

PAGEANT OF ULENHALL.

Producer .. The Rev.T.H.Evans F.R.G.S.

Coventry Cathedral Choir.

SCENE 1 The dawn of Christian faith.

Historical characters   Players

Ullen   Celtic Chieftain   Arthur H.Ashley
Brimola   His wife,   Ethel Trimble
Condo   Ullen's Messenger   Eric Taylor
Dona   Celtic Moot Harpist   Tony Taylor
Mafanva   Ullen's Body Guard   Peter Roden
Treforus   Celtic Monk Missioner   Tom Brokenshire
Davydd   Celtic Lay.Cross Bearer David Salmons
Waga   A Saxon Thane   Elvin Royall
Ceiros   Waga's Wife   Margaret Tolley
Irola   Waga's daughter   Anita Royall
Tirolma   Irola's young child   Timothy Royall
Holaner   Irola's elder son.   Howard Tolley

SCENE 2 The establishment of Barrells.

John Barrells. Lord of Barrells. John Summers
Franciscus Barrells. Lady of Barrells. Joan Phillips
Hugo Barrells. The Artist of Barrells. Brian MacKenna

Alsia. Elder daughter of Barrells. Betty Marshall
Elinore. Youngest daughter of Barrells. Anthea Hopkins

Mary Christian. Lady of Botley Manor. Grace Summors
Cossetta. House Maid of Barrells. Susan Vaughan.

Delsie Northerne. Lady of Apsley Manor. Winefred Richmond

Symon Bott. Village Reeve & Churchwarden. George Burgess
Marie Bott. his daughter. Gwen Burgess.

SCENE 2 .. continued ..

Argentel Witch. The witch of Dean's Green Martha Fullwood

Lucilla Boyne. Matron Ford Hall. Joan Clayton
Roberta Harper. Village Stockman. Jim Salmon.
Edwardus Corbett. Village Pound Man. Fred Tolley.
Jacobus Salomon. The Packman. Albert Boll.

SCENE 3. The Story of Crowley Manor.

Thomas Crowley. A Yeoman of Crowley. Basil Tisor
Erica Crowley. Famous Butter Maker. Rosemary Summers.

Candida Heath. Mother of Archbishop. E. Mary Friend.

Nicholas Heath. Archbishop Heath of York. Richard Perkins.

Adel Fane. Dairy Mid of Crowleys. Lilian Boll.
Jonathan Hoyle. Dairy Man of Crowleys. Florrie Morgan.

Mark Tarlton. Goat Cheese Maker. Joyce Betterton.
Jacko Napo. Woodman of Crowleys. John Neil.

SCENE 4. Time of Culture at Barrells. The Luxborough period.

Lady Luxborough. Literary figure. Barbara Siddall-Jones.

Katherine Moorland. Writer. Monica Montgomery.
Ann Horrop Price. Barrells Cook. Amelia Archer.
Elizabeth Lane. House Keeper at Barrells. Evelyn Barratt.

Old Joe. Groom of Barrells. Fred Colley.
Selesta. Hair Dresser of Barrells. Marjorie Colley

Alna   Their daughter.   Jane Colley.
Robert Knight. Cashier of South Sea. Grahame Millward.

William Shenstone. Poet Writer. Kenneth Karl.
William Somerville. Poet Hunter. Joseph Lloyd.
Rev.William Holyoak. Dr. & Vicar. Rowland Sparks.
Rev.Richard Iago. Vicar of Snitterfield Thomas Walker.

SCENE 5 .. Famous horse people of the day who visited Barrells Stables.

Earl of Catherlough. Famous figure. Kenneth Lackenby
Countess of Catherlough. Kept Stables. Oldyth Lackenby
Fram Dolman. Catherlough Stables Trainer. Robin Prike.
Losser Hyde. Horse Doctor Catherlough Stables. Michael Taylor

Petta Hughes. Riding companion. Sheila Tomlin
Countess of Huntingdon. Visitor. Sylvia Barwell.
Elfreda Gascoigne. French Riding companion. Olive Smith
Casandra Patol. Trainer Huntingdon Stables. Sandra Lewis.
Cafmel Kine. Horse Doctor Huntingdon Stables. Diane Lewis.
Count Duroure. Killed at Mockley fence.
Lord Segrave. Apsley Manor.

SCENE 6 .. The great social era at Barrells.

Viscount Bolingbroke. Secretary of State to Queen Anne. Barrie Cooper.
Viscountess Bolingbroke. An able politician. Debbie Wells.
Lady Archer of Umberslade. Of social importance. Mary Cox

Hon.Bulecta Archer. Anti-social daughter. Joan Forster.
Jane Davies. The beauty of Moat Farm. Sheila Cox.
Lady Hertford, of Ragley. near neighbour. Peggy Putman.
Lottie Koss. German companion. May Hemmings.
Duchess of Somerset. Botanist at Barrells. Madeline Jameson.

Hon.Elsa Brightwell. Companion to Duchess. Dora Forster.
The Lady Walter Manny. The Mannies of Apsley Manor.

SCENE - 7 .. The generous family at Barrells.

William Newton. Squire of Whately Hall. Bernard Duckworth

Isabet Newton. Established a tradition. Irene Clack.
Ruth Newton. An acknowledged scholar. Jannette Clack.
Thomas Henry Bodwin Newton. Built the Day School, Parish Church. Vicarage and Coffee House. Peter Wild.

Dordella Newton. Friend of the afflicted. Doris Amey.
Honora Thursfield. Wife of first Vicar. Esther Tomlin.
Lottie Courts. First Mistress Paid School. Mary Pugh.

SCENE 7 o. continued ..

Susana Dugar. Village Post Mistress. Freda Earl.
Amelia Batchelor. Village Dress Maker. Mavis Tomlin
Felicita Horn. Village Herb Seller & Evelyn Doctor Tasker

Jane Trott. Door to door Vendor. Jillian Summers
Thomas Franklin. Sexton & Parish Clerk. James Tasker

Archibald Dodds. Penny Farthing Cyclist. Austin Taylor.

-o-o-

The names and original characters are taken from the registers of the Old Chapel, The Visitor's Book of Barrells, kindly lent by Captain R.A. Homfray of Oxford.

-o-

ORDER OF GRAND FINALE & MARCH PAST VISITOR'S STAND

Group 1. Celtic Group
2. Establishment at Barrells
3. Crowley Manor Story
4. Times of Culture at Barrells
5. Famous Horse People at Barrells
6. Great Social Period at Barrells
7. The Newton era at Barrells.

Day School May Pole Dancers
Hampton in Arden Folk Dancers
Veteran Cars Parade
Old Bostock & Wombolls Circus Engine
The North Warwickshire Hunt
Parade of London Fashion Models.

Expression of Thanks.
I feel very humble when I think of the wonderful response to what appeared at first to be an impossible task. The marvellous response makes one feel proud of the friendship of all the Players, Stage Managers, Chroniclers, Dress Designers and Dress Makers, all who paid for the hire of costumes and everyone who so willingly helped.

T.H.Evans.

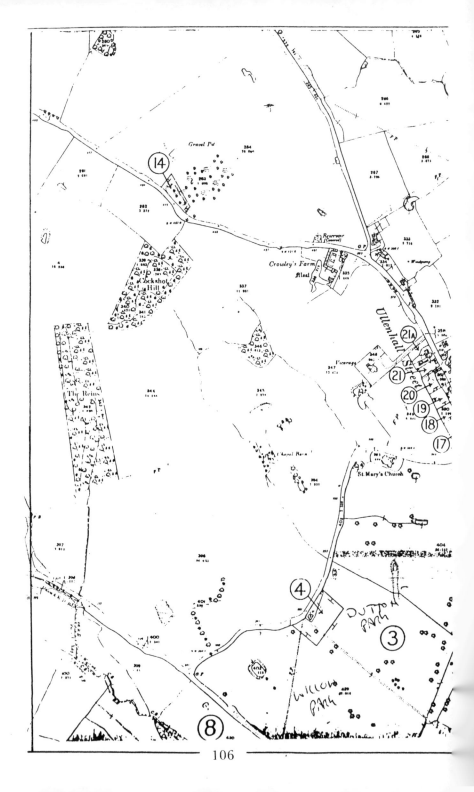

Gravel Pit

⑭

Crowley's Farm

Cockshot Hill

The Reins

Ullenhall Street

Vicarage

㉑A

㉑

⑳

⑲

⑱

⑰

Chapel Barn

St Mary's Church

④

DUTTON PARK

③

WILLOW PARK

⑧

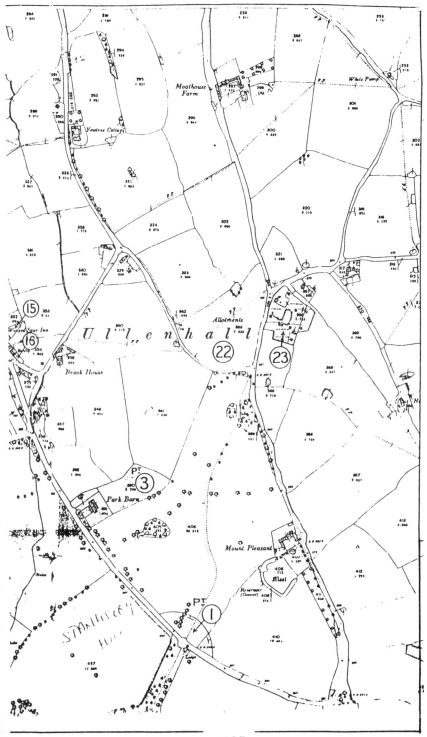

APPENDIX

CONVEYANCE OF STREET PIECE, ULLENHALL, 1863
Presented by Mr. Philip Styles from papers left by the late Mr. F.W.B. Yorks, 20 January 1970.

14 November 1863

Conveyance from the Reverend Thomas Jones clerk, perpetual curate of Bearley, with the consent of his patron, the Reverend Edward Dominic Geoffrey Martin Kirwan clerk, vicar of Wootton Wawen, also of his bishop and ordinary Henry bishop of Worcester, and Charles Thomas archbishop of Canterbury in whose province the curacy is situated, and of the Governors of Queen Anne's Bounty for the maintenance of poor clergy, to Mary Newton of Barrels Park widow, Thomas Henry Goodwin Newton of the Middle Temple, London, barrister, and the Reverend William Newton of York clerk in orders, for £246 10s 6d paid by the said Mary, Thomas and William Newton to the said Governors, of a piece of land called Street Piece containing 2 acres 2 roods 22 perches in Ullenhall in the parish of Wootton Wawen, numbered 481 on the Tithe Commutation Map for the said hamlet, with the following recitals:

i   a conveyance, dated 6 and 7 October 1780, from William James gentleman and Mary his wife, with the consent of the said Governors, to Daniel Collins clerk then curate of Bearley (reciting that on 14 May 1771 the Governors had agreed to augment the curacy with £200, that on 12 December 1771 they had agreed to augment the curacy with a further £200, and that in 1780 the said Governors had agreed to augment the curacy with a further £200 in conjunction with Mary Countess Dowager Gower who had given the like sum of £200 from the estate of the late Thomas earl Thanet; and reciting that it had been ordered by the Governors that the total sum of £800 should be laid out in the purchase of lands) of certain lands, containing the piece above-mentioned, for the perpetual augmentation of the said curacy:

ii   an act of parliament of 2 and 3 Victoria whereby it was enacted that in a case where a benefice had been augmented, with the consent of the Governors, with land outside the parish of such a benefice, it would be lawful for the incumbent thereof, with the consent of his patron, ordinary and the archbishop in whose province the benefice lay, to sell the said land, the proceeds of which sale would go to the said Governors:

iii   a memorandum of agreement of 27 June 1862 whereby the said Thomas Jones had contracted to sell the land above-mentioned to William Newton, who had died on 24 November 1862, having made a will with codicil, dated 22 June 1861 and 22 November 1862 respectively, whereby he devised his estate called Barrels in Ullenhall and the land which he intended to purchase from the said Thomas Jones, to his wife the said Mary Newton, his sons the said Thomas Henry Newton and William Newton, and trustees, directing that should the said purchase not be completed at the time of his death, the money for it should be paid out of his personal estate:

iv   a release, dated 30 March 1863, from the said trustees of any trusts or powers under the said will.
Plan annexed showing the said land to be bounded on the south by the road from Ullenhall to Henley, and by land of William Newton on every other side.

Signed: Thomas Jones, Edward Dominick Geoffrey Martin Kirwan, H. [bishop of] Worcester, C.T. [archbishop of] Cantuar', T.H. Goodwin Newton. Five red seals applied with the papered seals of the Governors, bishop and archbishop suspended on tags.

Witnesses: Geo. Aston cashier and accountant at the Bounty Office Dean's Yard Westminster, Chris. Hodgson treasurer of the same, Edward Cooper land agent of Henley-in-Arden, C.J. Furlong minister of Trinity Church Boulogne France, Alfred C. Hooper solicitor of Worcester, and John Burden solicitor and secretary to the archbishop 27 Parliament Street Westminster.

Three membranes.

Probate inventory of the goods of Richard Dale, blacksmith, of Ullenhall, 1615.

An inventory of all the goods & chattels late Richard Dale's of Ullenhall deceased taken and praised the eighth day of September in the yeare of our lord God 1615 by us, John Court, Nicholas Knight.

Imprimis in *the Haule* one long table with a frame, thereto belonginge, on square table with a frame, on forme, five plancks, benches, four shelves & on cheire
13s.4d.

Item on brasse pan, on great cawthern, three little kettels, on dabnit & on pot   32s.

Item fifteene peeces of pewter   10s.

Item on landiron, on pot, hangings, on old salt tub, stools and such small implements
2s.

Item in *the little chamber* on joyned beedsteed, on joined truckle bed, and foure coffers   21s.

Item on fetherbed, on wolbed, two coverlets & on duble twilly   38s.

Item his apparrell   13s.4d.

Item on paire of flaxen sheetes, 2 payre of hempton sheets, and five hurden sheets
35s.

Item on flaxen tablecloth, tow hurden tablecloths, on dussen of hempton table napkins, three pillowbears, on towel and eight els of hurden cloth   20s.

Item two fether pillowes, on fether bolster & on old bolster   6s.

Item in *the soller over the chamber* tow bedsteeds, tow flock beds, tow pillowes and on bolster, tow dubble twillies, tow old coverlets & on blanket   32s.

Item thre coffers, on cheese shelf, on chese cratch, an old barrell, on otmeale whisket, on winnowinge sheet, certayne bags, cheeses & other smale implements there   22s.

Item in *the buttery* on joyned cubbard, tow barrells, on lome, on churne, milk cans, on saw and other implements   15s.

Item in *the boulting house* on kneding skeele to make dough in, two lomes, on punning trough & other implements   10s.

Item in *the kichin* three wheeles, on ax, on bill, on spade, on forme, on tewtaw & other implements   5s.

Item in the shop one paire of smithes bellis   28s.

Item on handfild   50s.

Item on coltrough   2s.

Item on grindelstone   6d.

Item sixe hammers, three paire of toungs, five files, on paire of pinsons, five prichels, bickhorne and certayne stock and weights   15s.

Item on vice   4s.

Item timber, stocks, a pigs trough & wood	8s.
Item certaine muck	6s.8d.
Item certayne hay	£4
Item corne in the barne of all sorts	£4.10s.
Item on nage and tow colts	£5
Item tow hogs	26s.8d.
Item five kyne	£10
Item geese & poultry	5s.
Item tow yeare old calves	40s.
Item hempe	5s.
Item five shepe	25s.
Item the wood growing in Hawkridge Coppis which Richard Dale did buy of his mother and paide her for it to be fell att his pleasure	£6

Exhibited 24 November 1615

Summa totalis £58.   6d.

1873

10th June

The Birmingham morning news says that on this day (the same day on which a severe thunderstorm occurred in Coventry) a perfect tornado seems to have visited some of the rural villages in central Warwickshire. The following particulars have been supplied by William Rushton and William Fieldhouse of Ullenhall, both of whom witnessed it and narrowly escaped injury on the estate of Mr Newton, Barrells Hall. Large trees were blown down, torn up by the roots and the branches carried a considerable distance by the force of the hurricane. A farm house was unroofed and even the lead gutters were torn up and carried away. In the little village of Ullenhall the homestead of Mr Hawker suffered serious injury. The house was unroofed, cowsheds and piggeries were destroyed, many of the trees in the garden and orchard torn up and some of them carried to a distance of 200 yards, two straw ricks were carried bodily across a wheat field and the whole neighbourhood around was strewn with fragments and debris of various kinds. Mr Hawker saw the whirlwind coming towards his farm. "The air was thick with broken boughs" he says "and the roar sounded like the cawing of thousands of noisy rooks". With the great presence of mind, Mr Hawker called his family and servants from the house and conveyed them to a shed at the rear, believing that the house itself, which stood exposed to the full fury of the tornado, must suffer very considerably. Nor was he mistaken. Windows were smashed in, and much damage was done to the roof and interior of the dwelling. In Oldbury Wood, oak trees were uprooted, other trees were slivered into splinters and carried long distances. The farm of Mr Tom Hawker, brother to the gentleman just named, was also visited by the storm. The house was unroofed and cross-tiles of some new outbuildings were carried away and a straw rick was scattered far and wide. On the farm of Messrs Scroxton and Brookes, a good deal of damage was also done. The total damage, so far as it is known will represent several thousands of pounds sterling. Fortunately no loss of human life is reported, and the number of sheep and cattle destroyed is very small, considering the violence of the hurricane. One of the oak trees uprooted was 3ft 2" in diameter and 9ft 8" in circumference, and turf 16ft by 12ft was carried away with it. The "oldest inhabitant" of Ullenhall cannot remember a previous storm of such violence and the youngest will never forget it.